Sanford W. Berman
Atlanta, July, 1964

TH

OF THE

THE *HEART*
OF THE *FOREST*

ADRIAN COWELL

ALFRED · A · KNOPF : NEW YORK

1961

L. C. catalog card number: 60–53235

THIS IS A BORZOI BOOK,
PUBLISHED BY ALFRED A. KNOPF, INC.

FIRST AMERICAN EDITION

FOR

my Parents

AUTHOR'S NOTE

THIS BOOK is an account of an unexplored part of the forest of Amazonia, and the strange character of this land has had its effect on the chapters that follow. In the region of Xingu there are more than a dozen Indian tongues and most communication is in Portuguese, which the pacified tribesmen have picked up in a curious bastard form. This is not always easy to translate; words and phrases have peculiar local meanings and significance. The home town or village of any man is his "Cuiaba" because the first civilized people to enter the region came from the Mato Grosso capital of Cuiaba; Brazilians and all foreigners are "Caraiba," an Indian word for the Carib group of tribes which means invader; the Portuguese adjective "tough" in certain senses almost signifies "good" because strength and durability are essential to Indian life in the forest; and all conversation is accompanied by a sort of wild but joyous pantomime that is essential to its understanding. There is, for example, no other method of naming the time of the day than pointing at a place in the sun's course across the sky, and variations of intonation are the only way of expressing degree. "Good," "Gooood," and "Goooooooood" mean entirely different things. In this manner, a primitive Indian people who naturally speak in short sentences and without much refinement of meaning, have created a strange pidgin Portuguese which, to a certain extent, is a literal translation of the moods and assumptions of their own language. Some of the warriors of the Kamayura tribe are reasonably easy to understand, but the words are really no more than civilized envelopes for Indian meanings that require experience to interpret. With the Txukahamae tribe—very primitive and only recently contacted—it can take five minutes to establish a single point. "Feather pass when sick. Other. There. Woman works child. Kill turkey. Woman pain, pain. Kill more turkey. Man. Turkey strong. Child die," was a typical Txukahamae explanation of a tribal custom.

Clearly this primitive language raises problems for a book. Something must be done to make the talk readable and yet any major rewriting would remove the last chance of conveying the moods and inherent assumptions of the Indian brain. As these are the clue to practically everything that happened, I was faced with a choice between readable conversation and "writing out" the reason for noting it in the first place. The result was a compromise. The meaningless and wandering passages have been omitted, but the rest of the dialogue has been left as crude and rough as it really was. The product is somewhat ugly, but it is true to the language and gives the reader a chance to make something of it for himself.

Another problem has been the eerie, intangible nature of everything that was happening amongst the Indians. Explanations of many of the events are the purest guesswork and so they have all been described from the author's personal viewpoint. This is an inexperienced and amateur one, but inasmuch as its scope is roughly apparent, it would appear to be the safest foundation.

On the journey I relied entirely on the immense kindness of the Brazilians and Indians mentioned in the pages that follow, and though few of them can read a book, they will be pleased to hear that my gratitude has been recorded in one. Sincere thanks are also due to the Indian Protection Service, the President and the personnel of the Central Brazilian Foundation, the Brazilian Air Force, Mr. Callado of the Correio da Manha, Mr. Jose de Meira Pena of the Brazilian Foreign Office, the British Embassy in Rio de Janeiro and Mr. Desmond Cole. As most of these are Brazilians, some may feel slightly hurt that their countrymen and government are not always presented in a favourable light. But in writing a book about an outstanding Brazilian achievement it would be niggardly to conceal the truth and thus minimize the difficulties that had to be overcome. Criticisms are always the comments of Brazilians themselves and are never anything but kindly meant.

For valuable help in the preparation of the manuscript I would finally like to record my thanks to Mr. John Elsom, Mr. Patrick Allen, Miss Elinor Murphy, Mr. Henry Robbins, and the members of the Oxford and Cambridge Expedition to South America. Most of the photographs—and all the better ones—were taken by the expedition's photographer, John Moore, when he visited Capitao Vasconcelos for a fortnight.

The map on page 2 has been drawn from a section of the American Geographical Society map 1:5,000.000. The two other maps have been drawn from sections of USAF aeronautical charts 1:1,000.000. All these maps are reproduced by courtesy of the institutes concerned.

The quotation from Bertrand Flornoy's book *Jivaro* appears on page 207 by permission of Elek Books, Ltd.

A. C.

CONTENTS

INTRODUCTION   3

PART I: ORLANDO'S CUIABA

1. THE MORNING OF THE AEROPLANE   13
2. HUNTING   27
3. ORLANDO'S CUIABA   41
4. POISON FISHING   51
5. THE LITTLE QUARUP   59
6. KALUANA   71
7. CLAUDIO ARRIVES   85
8. DEATH WISH   93
9. TAMUAN   103
10. THE END OF AUGUST   113

PART II: THE CENTRO EXPEDITION

11. THE EXPEDITION SETS OUT   119
12. THE PLACE OF THE BLACK PUMAS   128
13. THE SERINGUEIRO KILLINGS   140
14. CUTTING THE TRAIL   152
15. WHY THE PUMA KILLS   169

Contents

16. THE LAST EL DORADO   180
17. THE RAPIDS AND BELOW   193
18. SEX AND THE DYING OF THE TRIBES   200
19. MEN WHO EAT EARTH   211
20. THE END   226

Glossary of Indian Tribes   237

ILLUSTRATIONS

Mount Roraima	FOLLOWING PAGE	50
Orlando Villas Boas		50
The River of Deaths		50
The main hut at Capitao Vasconcelos		50
The hunting country of the Kuluene Forest		50
Bebcuche pounding rice		50
Bebcuche winnowing		82
The "Fawcett" grave		82
"The Seven Cities"		82
Kamayura tribesmen		82
The Kamayura village		82
The traditional Urua dance		82
Kamayura warriors preparing for wrestling		114
A Kamayura warrior		114
Ceremonial wrestling		114
An Aweti warrior		114
A mission child of the dying Bororo tribe		114
Two Kamayura boys pounding mandioca		114
The Dance of the Dead		114
A Trumai boy during initiation		114
Orlando's scissors are used during initiation		146

A boy drinking the initiation poison 146
He tickles his throat and liquid pours out 146
Dilton de Motta with a Suya pot 146
Preparing the canoes 146
The men who clubbed the seringueiros 146
Siriri, one of the Juruna warriors 178
Typical seringueiros 178
Claudio Villas Boas 178
Rauni the Txukahamae 178
Aligning the trace to the Centro 178
The Geographical Center of Brazil 178
Claudio at the Txukahamae encampment 178
A Txukahamae hut 178
Mengrire 210
Txukahamae boy 210
A mission Indian cracking and eating nuts 210
An Indian raincoat 210
A Kamayura woman making a basket 210

MAPS

PAGE
The North Mato Grosso 2
Tribes in Orlando's Cuiaba 12
Tribes in the area of the Centro Expedition 118

THE *HEART* OF THE *FOREST*

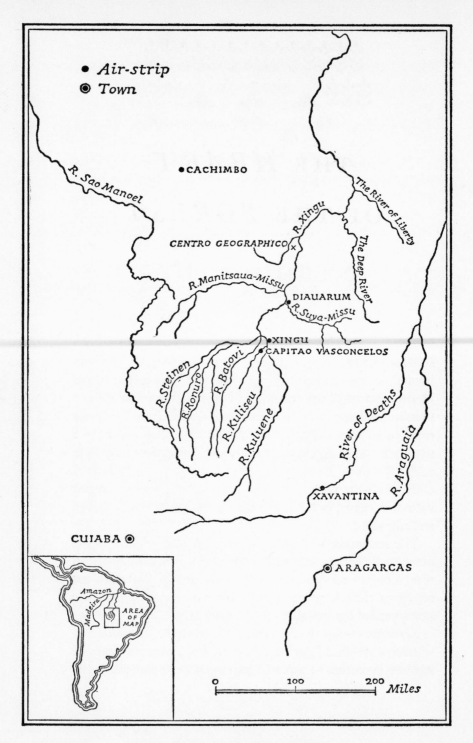

THE NORTH MATO GROSSO

INTRODUCTION

IN DECEMBER 1957, I made a journey along the northern border of the Amazon jungle. Stanley Jeeves and John Moore who had been travelling with me on an Oxford and Cambridge Expedition to South America suggested that the three of us should leave the main group of our party for a month in order to march towards an intriguing mountain called Roraima. This box-like massif in the forest had sheer cliffs two thousand feet in height and was the world's largest natural fortress. It had long had a reputation for isolation and mystery.

The mountain was first discovered in the middle of the nineteenth century, at a time when every year brought fresh revelations of science. This sudden finding of a plateau cut off by its cliffs from the rest of the world since prehistoric times excited the imaginations of explorers.

Zoologists—developing Darwin's theory of evolution—wondered whether Roraima could conceal examples either of separate evolution or arrested zoological development in the

form of prehistoric animals. Other people talked about diamonds and lost cities, and finally Sir Arthur Conan Doyle
summed up all this speculation in his novel *The Lost World*.
In this, Professor Challenger discovered pterodactyls, dinosaurs, and ape-men upon the summit. But what is particularly impressive about the book is the description of the
mountain itself. Doyle presented it as nature's last hiding-
place, surrounded by nature's entire battery of defences. The
mystery and strength almost hiss at you out of the pages.
The very mountain seems to have a malevolent being.

The three of us who were to make the journey had read
The Lost World and possessed widely differing opinions. "I
don't believe," John said, "that any mountain can be as powerful and sinister as that. Mountains are rock and rock doesn't
have character." Stanley, however, had been on climbing expeditions in the Alps and Himalayas. "Mountains have more
character than people," he argued. "You can hear them talking to your boots as you climb."

The three of us travelled by truck to the cattle town of
Boa Vista, by plane to the diamond mine of Suapi, and then
by bullock to an Indian hut that faced the mountain across
sixty miles of dividing valley. After two days of incessant
bargaining, in which the unusually civilized Indians told us
that porters had inexplicably become expensive at the time
of our arrival and considered dried milk (to be provided by
us) part of their traditional diet, a price was agreed. Then
we learned that the tribe belonged to a strange Christian sect
called the Angelicans. A Negro preacher had passed through
some years before on his way from the jungles of the north
and now that they were converted, these savannah Indians
could not work on Saturdays. As neither we nor they had
kept track of the calendar the argument was one of infinite
possibilities. The calabash of mandioca "beer" passed from
hand to hand; the bargaining continued late into the night.

Finally we set out at noon on the next day. There were three of us—John, Stanley and myself, five porters, six women, three boys, and two babies that were still sucking. As we walked the Indians uttered a long-drawn, high-pitched cry that echoed about the hills—"Roraaaaaaaiiima." This was taken up by the others with "Haaaaaiiiiaaaas" and "Aaaaaaiiiieees" and wailing repetitions of the mountain's name, so that, trudging towards the massive climax it made upon our horizon, we were almost forced to sink into the romantic atmosphere of *The Lost World*.

When we had been back in civilization, the three of us had often found it difficult to appreciate why so many men had been deceived by dreams or fables in the land of Amazonia: why the treasure seekers had believed in El Dorado, why Fawcett had pursued his cities of Atlantis, and why a mountain should be regarded as anything but an outsize conglomeration of sedimentary rock. But approaching Roraima the matter was different. The sands of civilization were no longer about our ostrich eyes. It was not man that was the lord of nature but nature that was the master of man. We looked at the mountain with awe. We noted that the streams we crossed were dangerous because of the waters that flowed from its cliffs, that the clouds in all our skies were courtiers to Roraima's summit, and that the agony of the hard bare hills that writhed under our feet seemed somehow to acknowledge the overlordship of the monster above.

For the first days, the mountain itself was hidden in great banks of cloud that blew up from the Atlantic Ocean. But one morning the sky cleared and the tableland became distinct. From the level of the lower hills at roughly five thousand feet Roraima rose normally for the next two thousand; but then—quite suddenly—the swelling ceased and along the entire eight-mile face of the mountain were sheer cliffs that soared up two thousand feet more. The summit was a surprisingly level line broken by craggy crenellations. The walls were black, striped with the red and white of exposed sandstone, and a third of the way along there was a "rift" valley, half a mile in width, that cut the mountain in two.

On the fifth day out, we began the final ascent. It was dawn and the mountain was clear of cloud so that we could see the only ledge like a drawbridge slanting to the top, and a cloud formation as strange as the mountain itself lying in the rift valley below us. Some freak of the winds had twisted the clouds into a long and permanent line of vapour; like a lizard's tongue, it flicked in and out of the valley's mouth and periodically blew a puff as a smoker blows a ring. Then, as we began to approach the belt of white tree skeletons that encircled the mountain, the mist came down, sickly grey, like poison gas over a war cemetery. It swirled around the many spiky plants known as "Christ's Crown of Thorns" and amongst the grotesque spiders that were spinning webs from plant to plant.

We climbed steadily. A light drizzle began to fall. Another hour and we were under the cliffs and in the rain forest. Thick, sickly mosses clung to every surface; distorted, ugly fungi sprang from every tree. The pools of water were black, the fallen rocks from the cliff face formed caverns that were too dank even for the snakes, and the trees and bushes were twisted in agonized misshapen forms. We were glad, ninety minutes later, to climb on to the mountain ledge.

There, shrouded in mist, we could just make out the wall of cliff to our right and its plunging face to our left. Once we sighted a great jet of water spouting from the rock face; another time we passed under a waterfall that had fallen so far that it reached us as spattered drops of rain. We climbed and climbed and climbed and, not far from the middle of the day, we passed from the ledge on to Roraima's summit.

There was nothing to see. Just black crags appearing and

disappearing in cloud and rain. The mountain had vanished and, as it grew cold and the night and the rain came down, we put up our tent and crawled into sweaters and sleeping bags. But at dawn next day there was warmth and not a cloud in the sky. We scrambled out over a mass of rocks to the nearest block of high ground and looked out upon a landscape of the moon, an immense saucer of contorted, ugly, and convulsed black rock. Everything was of stone for miles in every direction, and the stones were piled and carved as if a million demoniac rock artists had contrived the decoration of a Titan's torture chamber. There were huge formations eroded by the winds that tore about the mountain. We saw shapes like a thumbscrew, a crippled camel, a tortoise without its head, and a pig with a bloodsucker clinging to its back. One gallery, cut into the rock, had the curved roof and pillars of a side aisle in a Gothic church; with gargoyles more ugly than those of Notre Dame, it seemed an appropriate setting for a mediæval Black Mass. "Happen you had all this in England," said Stanley, "you'd make a right lot of money letting folks in at sixpence a time." It was indeed nature's own chamber of horrors. Something of the essence of Amazonia was in the scale of those enormous rocks and in the cruelty of that black landscape.

Later in the day, we discovered that the two streams that drain the central saucer from opposite directions plunge into rock fissures close together in the centre. There they disappear in a series of deep caves till they emerge—presumably —in the waterspouts we had seen hundreds of feet lower down in the cliff face. Stanley, who had spent fifteen years exploring the potholes of England, argued that if the rocks of the summit could be so eroded by wind and rain, then the passage of vast quantities of water since the beginning of time must have hollowed out caverns in the centre of the mountain. We had seen the streams go in and come out, and had deduced that several of the gorges on the surface were in fact caverns with roofs that had fallen in. It was logical to assume that part of the mountain was a maze of passages, wells, and cathedral-like caves. A Brazilian geologist had told us that the diamonds which have been washed down the rivers of British Guiana, Venezuela, and Brazil over the centuries, all stemmed from a mountain core somewhere in the Roraima range. It was possible that this cave cross-section of the mountain would offer a clue to the "diamond pipe," or reveal a place where a few heavy stones had been trapped as the water flowed by.

Sitting in the swinging mist of that eerie, moonlike world, it was hard to halt reason in its slide to fantasy and not feel that we too belonged to all that tradition of Amazonian adventurers who had tried to tear secrets and fortunes from the forest. We had neither the equipment nor the necessary food supplies for a proper exploration. But discovery was before us.

Next morning, we made a preliminary survey, and the result was that Stanley, our climbing expert, slipped on a belay and fell thirty feet on to the rocks below, fracturing his foot. We rescued him and then considered the situation. With a difficult descent before us, almost no food, and aeroplanes and medical help over a week away, the return journey promised to be dangerous. "Right silly I'd look," Stanley said glumly, "if the boys at the Fell and Rock Club in England knew about this. They'd burst all the Yorkshire potholes with laughing."

Next day, Stanley crawled and slid his way on the rump of his trousers down three thousand feet to the camp in the foothills. The jagged rocks and close-fitting jungle made a stretcher and our attempt at pick-a-back impossible. A descent that should have taken two and a half hours took him ten, and he eventually became so blind with exhaustion that both his hands and both his knees passed over a poisonous snake before we saw and killed it. On any other mountain we should have left him on the summit, giving the fracture time to rest in the week that it would take to bring a horse within reach of the foothill camp. In the case of Roraima it was a decision that not one of us was prepared to consider. "It's an inhospitable sort of place," Stanley said, "all angles and hard lines. No trees or animals. Just stubbly coarse bushes, and insects that are black, and rain and cold and no fire. There's something about it . . ."

In the hungry days that followed, as we sat in the camp watching the high smoke signals that marked our Indians travelling for supplies and horses, and on the morning when we finished the last of our food, we were very conscious that there was "something about it." We were off the mountain with our backs towards it, and yet its presence dominated all our senses. Of course the mountain was not associated with the spirit of Amazonia, and, of course, the forest had not retaliated because we had tried to explore one of its last secret places, but Roraima's power and size had become so dominant in our minds that it did not seem ridiculous to talk of such things. We sat on our hillside on the northern watershed of the Amazon basin gazing out over a great expanse of primeval forest that stretched for two thousand miles across South America. Its size and strength seemed almost overpowering. "If this is just the edge of the forest," said Stanley, "then there must be something right big in the middle." We speculated about it. Would there be diamonds? Could it conceal some unknown Amazonian drug? Would such an elemental monster as the forest have an unusual being—a soul or spirit—at its centre? We decided that one of us, one day, would try to find out. "It should be an interesting sort of place," I said. "I suppose we should be looking for the Heart of the Forest."

"I don't know about hearts," was Stanley's hungry reply,
"but I know one thing. There'd be vegetation. Soggy and
dripping. Like wet cabbage," he added wistfully, "just out of
the saucepan."

For a guess, Stanley's comment was remarkably accurate.

PART · I

Orlando's Cuiaba

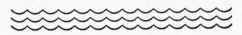

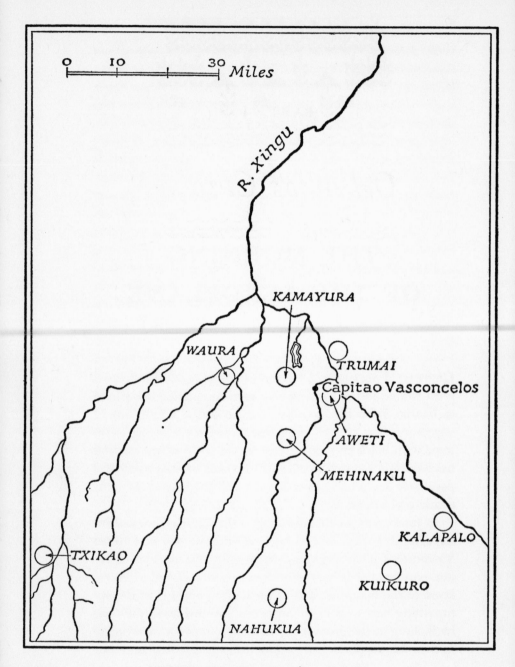

TRIBES IN ORLANDO'S CUIABA

1

THE MORNING
OF THE AEROPLANE

CAPITAO VASCONCELOS is an outpost of civilization—a great wound in the jungle where man has blasted out a hole to live in. From the main hut, the view is of a long line of vegetation that cuts off the horizon, and the clearing is littered with black and rotting tree trunks lying where axe and fire have laid them. The whole compound has the harsh and peculiarly gaunt outlines of a bomb site. It is one of the most desolate places on earth.

In June 1958, at the beginning of the Centro Geographico Expedition, I spent several hours of utter despair at Capitao Vasconcelos. That morning—as on every Vasconcelos morning—my hammock was tied between the wall and a central beam in the main hut, and as I swung to and fro in the approaching heat of a Brazilian noon, I whiled away the time by looking at the grooves my hammock ropes were wearing in their log supports. Only a few weeks had passed since our arrival and already a distinct curved line was running round the logs and cutting into the wood. Perhaps—if our exile continued—my weight and the boredom of this life would one day pull these ropes right through the last inch of wood and the logs would come tumbling down. It was a new and welcome idea in the tedium of forest life and my mind wandered round it wasting not a single morsel. Perhaps the roof would fall down even before the logs. Perhaps the logs were already riddled with termites. Perhaps . . . Like driftwood on a jungle river, thought tumbled and floated with the current of our day as we waited and listened for the one thing that could bring change to Vasconcelos. We were three men hoping to leave on an expedition into the jungle and yet supplies were barely adequate for our base camp. For a fortnight the menu had been rice and beans and though, occasionally, one of the two was omitted, this variation was limited in its permutations. There could be rice. There could be beans. There could be both. The menu was our Vasconcelos gamble —an intriguing element of chance in the monotony of jungle life.

And then, quite suddenly, all our lethargy vanished. A sound so faint that it could barely be heard, seemed to materialize in the eastern part of the sky. I listened. It gradually swelled into a powerful roar coming down over the jungle.

"The Dakota!" Juan shouted ecstatically into the roof. "The Dakota!" he shouted again, and the three of us rushed out of our log-and-thatch hut and hurried up towards the airstrip.

In front, Orlando Villas Boas brushed aside the foliage. Orlando's small stocky figure was completely naked, except for a pair of bottle-green shorts roughly assembled from camouflaged parachute silk. "I told you," he said over his shoulder. "If you wait, aeroplanes come."

Behind him, Juan and I followed together. Juan was a

short fussy man just under forty. I was a tall, gangling foreigner with an incipient beard.

When the Dakota eventually landed, we were standing—
three urgent and dusty men—at the fuselage doorway. Suddenly the door swung aside, and the pilot appeared.

"Cargo," he said wincing in the heat. "I have cargo for
Capitao Vasconcelos." And the three of us breathed a sigh of
relief that lasted till Orlando walked over to the freight com-
partment and looked inside. His shoulders drooped, his legs
sagged at the knees, and all the weariness of our forest life
came back into his voice.

"Food," he said bitterly, "but no gasolene."

"It's always the same," Juan said to the pilot. "When you
bring gasolene there is no food. So we have to send boats
down river to fish. Now there is food and we have no gasolene. It has been happening," he said with emphasis, "for a
long time."

Indeed, to my knowledge it had been going on for seven
months, ever since Juan and Orlando had started to await
the supplies of their expedition in January 1958. Every week
they had gone to the airstrip to inquire about food when they
had gasolene, and gasolene when they had food. Every week
they had hoped to leave the week after. It was such an inexplicable and recurrent tragedy that in my eyes the plane
had assumed the character of a gift-bearing but irresponsible
Greek god. What really lay behind the delay, I was not to
discover for several weeks.

A short time later the aeroplane vanished into the sky and
we were left standing motionless on the airstrip. I could see
Juan looking at the vegetation, and it was almost as if we
could feel the enormous pressure of the jungle pounding in
on the outskirts of our clearing. Just as the Jews at Belsen
must have felt that a whole nation of armed hatred was
pressing in on the barbed wire of their cage, so we were con-

scious of the hundreds of miles of unexplored wasteland straining toward our vacuum in the trees. It was an ominous sensation that even penetrated into the hut, for when we returned, it was as dank and shadowed as an animal's lair. There were no windows, the floor was of trodden mud, and the place was filled with the sombre gloom of deep Amazonian jungle.

"You will see," Orlando said, waving his hands dramatically. "Aeroplanes are like pigeons. They always come back if you trust them."

Juan made no reply. "Things go round and round in my head," he said. "They go round and round." His eyelids flickered nervously, and first one hand and then another went up to smooth his face and little goatee. "I can hardly talk," he concluded, subsiding into his hammock.

As if driven by the same inexorable law, Orlando and I climbed into our hammocks as well. It was a moment of utter despair. The expedition would set out one day in the future—we were confident of that—but whether it would be seven days or seven months from now, there could be no way of telling. For though the plan was simple enough, the presence of mysterious and possibly unfriendly forces beneath the surface made it almost impossible to guess what would happen.

The sun climbed higher into the sky, the jungle began to creak and rustle under the midday heat, and one of the post's tame woodpeckers flew onto my hammock and fell asleep close to my nose. I settled down for a long day with my thoughts.

. . . .

I had first heard about the Centro Expedition when travelling through the Brazilian state of Mato Grosso toward the southern fringe of the Amazon forest, and even at that early stage all the past events of my previous few years had somehow seemed a preface to it. After finishing at Cambridge University, I had spent a year on the Oxford and Cambridge Far Eastern Expedition, which opened up the overland motor route from London to Singapore. Then, the Oxford and Cambridge Expedition to South America had brought me to the Amazon forest where we had spent a year travelling to places like Roraima and working in some of the undeveloped regions of the Amazon forest. Finally, the last stage of this second journey had brought me to Capitao Vasconcelos, and I had been intrigued by Villas Boas's plan for an expedition into the unexplored region of Xingu. I waited till I had known him for some weeks and then asked if I could join his party. "We are taking a dozen primitive Indians," was the reply, "so we should be able to cope with an Englishman as well." I was accepted; the long wait had begun.

At that time, the President of Brazil was gambling his career and straining his country's finances to build a new capital in the interior. Brasília, as he called it, was to be the master stroke that would change the future of his country. The capital would be moved into the strategic centre of the state and placed in a key position to develop the immense resources of Brazil. It would wrest the national mind from Rio de Janeiro and the coasts of the Atlantic to its great destiny in the undeveloped forests of Amazonia. Our expedition was to be part of this program. We were to canoe down the Xingu River and burn an airstrip at the exact geographical centre of Brazil.

The precise significance of this act would not be apparent to foreigners. For most Brazilians, the meaning is to be found in their nation's history and geography. Four hundred years earlier, Indian tribes had started fleeing before the attack of the conquistadors. They pressed deeper and deeper into the forest of Amazonia until they reached its almost impregnable centre at Xingu. There they turned to fight for their survival. To the east the Xavantes made their River of Deaths the frontier of civilization and killed every pioneer that crossed its banks; once it was said to have flowed scarlet for two days with the blood of an invading band. To the north, the Kayapo murdered every stranger, whether Indian or civilizado, that crossed their nomad patrol. And to the west, the Kayabi went down into legend as the Catmen who paint a black whisker on their faces for each white man they have ambushed.

As the rest of Amazonia was explored, this box of resistance had acquired definition and frontiers. It stood on a plateau roughly two thousand feet high, marked to the east by the River of Deaths, to the west by the St. Manoel River, to the south by a mountain range, and to the north by a drop in level to the alluvial plains of the Amazon basin. Down the centre, the Xingu River and its tributaries made a backbone that united the whole into a territory loosely known as "Xingu."

Many explorers before Orlando Villas Boas had tried to cross into this "Heart of the Forest." In 1941, seven men of a group led by Pimental Barbosa were found dead with war clubs under their naked bodies; before them, two missionaries; before that, a man was discovered in his hammock, with a stake thrust from his mouth to the back of his neck; and so on, back into history. From the south, the Xingu River had been descended as early as 1885 by the great German scientist, von den Steinen. He had been followed by Dyott and other explorers, who mainly limited themselves to the headwaters, but of these only half returned. They had collected information around the rivers, but none had been able to get inland from the waterways and none had been able to stay very long. Like a Forbidden City or Lost World, the territory between the River of Deaths and the St. Manoel River had remained a place of mystery and legend. The English explorer, Colonel Fawcett, even pointed out that though there were warlike tribes elsewhere in Amazonia, they were not so apparently organized into a defensive position. He argued that the Indians were satellites collected in a defensive screen around the city-civilization that had fathered the Incas and that had come from the lost continent of Atlantis. No one could disprove his theory because no one knew what was inside the box; in 1925, it was the only unexplored area on earth large enough to conceal a whole civilization. Fawcett and his companions went to look; they disappeared. Then, of the search parties, Albert de Winton and an Italian expedition vanished as well. By 1943, the great centuries of discovery had served to do no more than emphasize the mystery and impregnability of this strange citadel of the forest.

Then the beginning of change came with the Central Brazilian Foundation. This pioneer organization was created by the government to begin exploration from the air, and its primary expedition set out with three brothers, Orlando, Claudio, and Leonardo Villas Boas, in the vanguard. For the first time, aerial supply made a long-term expedition possible, and the brothers had begun to build a line of airstrips right across the forest. Over the fifteen years that followed, the government campaign to conquer the land had become virtually a personal one; soon, all expeditions had been led by one of the Villas Boas trio.

By 1958, Claudio was finishing the last emergency runway at Cururu. Six others lay diagonally across the forest. The general position was as if the British Isles had become virgin jungle and there were airstrips at Dover, London, Birmingham, Glasgow, Aberdeen, and Belfast, with the nearest civilizado settlement at Paris. Scattered across the rest of England, Ireland, Wales, and Scotland there would be more than a score of tribes of whom half were friendly to the Villas Boases but still killed other civilizados that they found on their frontiers. The other half were unpacified, and killed civilizados and other Indians indiscriminately.

The purpose of the Centro Expedition was to bring this work to some sort of climax. For years the Villas had been struggling towards the ultimate defeat of the forest, but because it was an indeterminate area with no obvious point like the South Pole for the flag raising of symbolic success, it had been hard for outsiders to appreciate what they were doing. Some government officials, therefore, conceived the plan of burning an airstrip at the exact geographical centre of Brazil. If an expedition could cut its way to a place chosen by a geographers' formula, it would demonstrate that Brazilians were capable of going to any point arbitrarily selected in the most dangerous area of Amazonia. And if that expedition could construct an airstrip on which President Kubitschek could land, it would symbolize man's victory over the powers of nature. Brazil would have conquered the greatest forest on earth.

That was the plan. But as I lay in my hammock throughout this gloomy day of the aeroplane, I was sadly aware that the theory of the expedition was modified by the character and aims of the men who were to lead it.

Some days after I had joined the party, Juan had given me my first clue. He was a kind, likeable man who had devoted much of his time to helping Orlando in his work with the Indians, but unfortunately his health was under strain. "It's the drugs that keep it in," he had told me. "I may look warm outside, Adriano, but inside my marrow and intestines are shivering with malaria. You cannot imagine it. My brain can hardly talk at all.

"I am cracking here, Adriano," he confided, hand on pelvis. "It may break soon and then everything will come out."

I was not completely surprised, therefore, when he asked mysteriously: "Why do you think the plane flew over last week without delivering supplies?"

I said I didn't know.

"It's because they don't like Orlando in the other party."

"But what party?"

"The party against us of course.[1] Against me and Orlando and the other Air Force officers who stop at Vasconcelos. Why do you think we were a whole month eating nothing but rice and beans? The pilots are in the President's party. They are spending Brazil into bankruptcy to build this new capital, Brasília. And what do we want it for? Rio de Janeiro is the most beautiful capital in the world. If we want to develop the interior, we should spend the money on roads. Instead, the first thing we do is to build a new capital in the jungle. Who else does that? Tell me, who else does that?"

I looked at Juan and tried to conceal my surprise. Wasn't it true that Brasília and its policy were tied up with the Centro Expedition? the expedition I had just joined?

"The Centro Expedition!" Juan's voice became dark and cynical. "Risk lives to make an airstrip in the middle of nowhere. What progress is that? And this progress business. Fat men in the Chamber of Deputies talking of the triumphant stride of Brazil into the magnificent future of the world. No one will come here for land for fifty years, maybe a hundred. They just buy and sell it in land speculation offices so that rich people get richer. Claudio Villas Boas once took some Indians to the President with new wounds from civilizado bullets. And the President said that everyone knew that he, the President, was a friend of the Indian, and that he

[1] At the time, the new capital was the subject of violent political controversy and there was a great deal to be said for both points of view.

would send a memorandum about it to the House of Deputies. Indians dying, he sends a memorandum. The President! Ha!

"It will be a fine expedition, Adriano, going to do something for which there is no point, and probably causing the death of Indians whose salvation is the only point worth while. Perhaps"—he became calmer—"it will never go. Probably it won't go at all."

At the time I had hoped it was the outburst of a sick man, but now after several weeks I realized that this was by no means a typical expedition, and Orlando no typical leader.

When I had first heard of Villas Boas I had thought of him through the imaginary portrait that serves everyone for an explorer: a man with huge, energetic limbs and a Roman nose brooding over a beard that would be black or russet. But he was, in fact, a little man—five feet and six inches—barefooted, bare-backed, with a pot belly lipping over his bottle-green pants. He might have been an attendant in a Turkish bath or a musician in a Paris salon. The only remarkable feature he had was a most powerful bearded and hawk-like face with many lines of hardship across it. It could have been a pirate's face, or perhaps even the face of a saint who had spent years in mortification. But, like the man's reputation, it gave no indication of the character within.

I knew that in the cities of Brazil, Orlando's name had captured public imagination much as Livingstone's had done in the nineteenth century. "He has lived in the jungle for fifteen years," people said. "He is like a saint with his Indians." But when I had mentioned something about this to Juan he had told me how three young anthropologists, two Swiss and one German, had flown into Vasconcelos. Whenever Orlando had spoken to the German, the latter had, to Juan's astonishment, sprung to his feet, clicked his heels, and replied at at-

tention. When it had been suggested that this was unneces-
sary in the forest, the German had been adamant.

"In my country we stand like this," he had said, "when we
talk to a man like that."

"This," Juan had concluded pointedly, "is not what Orlando is like."

On the other hand, I also knew that the prospectors and
adventurers of the Brazilian frontier-lands had their own
stories and rumours about the three exploring brothers
whom they jointly called the Villas. In the smoke and fumes
of their ramshackle bars, this name often acquired a sinister
meaning. "The place called Xingu," they would murmur
mysteriously into the second drink you bought them. "Aha,
that's a place for the devil to keep his black-breasted mis-
tresses. No one can get in except from the sky. And after the
Villas built their airstrips, not even the devil has been allowed in without a government paper. Some of the richest of
us have hired teku-tekus (small private aircraft), but they
have been chased all over the sky and arrested by those ——
the Air Force. Now we have no more aeroplanes. Other men
have gone to work at one of the six posts, but only the Villas
dare travel in the jungle and know how to handle the Indians. The place Xingu is like a private kingdom. In it"—
the voices would become hoarse with emotion—"are the
Mountains of Suffering. Gold! Oh my friend who buys me
drinks, what gold! Enough to buy up your little British Empire. Bartolomeu Bueno discovered it hundreds of years ago,
and when his grandson followed his directions, the Indians
got the party. It was a massacre and the secret was lost.
Now," the conclusion would come sadly with the end of the
drink, "now the Villas are looking for it all by themselves."

But after only a few months in Brazil, I had learned to be
cautious of pioneer tales. This one was probably a wild inter-

pretation of very dubious facts. Bartolomeu Bueno had certainly discovered gold, but there was no conclusive evidence that this had been in Xingu. It was also well known that money was the least of Orlando's ambitions; he had refused several high government posts, and the little income he had was devoted to his work for the Indians.

Much more curious were the apparently contradictory aims of Vasconcelos policy. Orlando Villas Boas was a salaried official of the Central Brazilian Foundation whose purpose was to develop the jungle in the name of national progress. Yet recently he had been seconded to the Indian Protection Service, whose officers were pledged to help the Indians. Every year they attempted to contact unpacified tribes under the principle, "Die if necessary, but never shoot back," and the whole spirit of their organization was to protect the tribesmen against the onslaught of civilization. It almost seemed as if the explorer had entered the jungle in the vanguard of a development campaign and had then changed his aims and ideals to work directly against the progress that had originally been his goal. If this was so then the purpose of the Centro Expedition was directly contradictory to the object of Orlando's life.

In fact, his work with the Indians was both hard to define and difficult to understand. Most historical examples of contact between our civilization and really primitive people have been of rapid death and ultimate extinction. In some cases, two hundred years of astonishing slaughter have ended with a slow improvement, but the few survivors are usually submerged within the stronger society. In Brazil at the beginning of this century two hundred and thirty tribes had survived the massacre to that date. By 1957, half of these had become extinct and the others had been reduced in number. In the particular circumstances of this part of the forest, the North Mato Grosso, the great Indian nation of the Bororos

had been pacified and cared for by some of the most gifted
and sympathetic Indian protectors the world has ever known.
And yet their numbers had fallen from 3,500 in 1900 to 150
in 1958. Extinction had almost swept over the tribe.

The strange thing was that these facts were known to Orlando; he had told me that the odds against him in his struggle to help the Indian were almost hopeless. He also believed
that the effect of his own arrival in Xingu had been the usual
pattern of shock to tribal life, followed by an increasing
death rate.

If that was so, and the Indians' only proven method of survival was to hide in the forest, then why, I wondered, was
Orlando trying to contact and pacify them? Like Alice in
Wonderland, everything in Xingu seemed to happen upside
down and back to front.

. . . .

By the end of the afternoon my head was spinning like a
bicycle wheel and, in my despair, I seemed, like Juan,
on the verge of some cerebral disease. Everyone at some
stage in his life feels on the doorstep of lunacy, and this
particular afternoon, surrounded by the powerful, almost
brooding, presence of the forest, the moment seemed to
have arrived for me. Something had to be done, something to preserve sanity. Slowly, I forced myself to realize
that to a complete outsider in one of the world's strangest
pockets of isolation, confusion was not altogether unexpected. A Scottish bishop is not at ease in a Cairo brothel and
an Eskimo is puzzled by cricket at Lords. And here everything was not only foreign to an Englishman, but also bound
up with a dark primitive Indian life separated by thousands
of years from the civilization of today. A solution for the
doubts raised by the delay of our aeroplane could not pos-

sibly come from reasoning but only from living the forest life till thoughts about it were from the inside and not those of the stranger. And thus in the heat of that Brazilian afternoon, the idea gradually developed—to live deeply the jungle life. To clutch the earth and learn through sense and instinct. It was not a particularly inspiring thought. One man, aged twenty-four, qualifications nil, experience non-existent, motives the lack of any alternative action. Presumably to sink into the forest existence, he should as far as possible suppress all bias—preconceived ideas, education, emotion, and individual philosophy; personal characteristics of this sort would deflect the understanding of what should be the mere cipher of a civilizado coming childlike to the jungle of Amazonia. And only at the end of it all should this man try to remember and analyse what he had seen. As a project it would have made Orlando snort and an anthropologist curl up in laughter, but for one person, at one point in time, marooned in the Amazonian jungle, it was to be the key to sanity. Even if the expedition never set out, I had a plan for the months ahead.

Dinner that night was served just before the sun went down and as I walked into the dining-hut I realized that already our delay had not been wasted. At Vasconcelos meals might vary but I now knew they never varied much. "Dinner," said Juan, "will be beans tonight," and he turned to look expectantly at me.

"You are wrong," I said, "the meal will be rice."

It was a pleasant game. One of us was sure to be right.

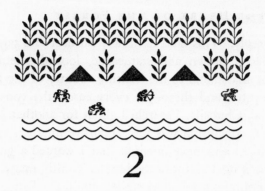

2

HUNTING

EVERY DAY SMALL parties of Indians come to Orlando's post from the eight pacified villages in the southern part of Xingu. Their settlements are placed at the end of trails in the jungle like spokes on the hub of the Vasconcelos wheel, and the journey varies from a few hours to several days. Sometimes canoes are used, and often parties of women and children come for the excursion, but usually it is the men alone who walk up from the river bank or stalk quietly out of the trees. They have the lithe, catlike physique of hunters.

Soon after my arrival at Capitao Vasconcelos I began to wonder if these men could be persuaded to teach a civilizado to stalk and live in the jungle, and on the day after the visit from the aeroplane, I decided to try my luck. I walked up to several groups of warriors as they sat on logs in the clearing and steered the talk cautiously round to the subject of beginners and hunting.

"There are deer and tapir in the forest," I hazarded. "Yes," was the reply. "This land has many fat deer and tapir." The Indian faces, brown and statuesque, looked solemnly out across the marshland to the hunting country of the Kuluene forest beyond, and there—in every case—the conversation would end. Clumsily, I searched about for another lead. But always the conclusion was the same. Eventually, I would be compelled to announce outright that I wanted a guide who would teach me to hunt in the jungle. To this, many warriors listened politely; some even smiled and looked encouraging; but always, at the crucial stage of the request, their eyes passed from the dark, ominous shape of the jungle to my own face. By contrast it must have looked exceptionally young and eager. Not even for a mammoth bribe—their expressions said—would an Indian take a beginner like this into the land of the snake and puma.

I was forced to lay my trap.

For several mornings, I made sure that I was seen walking in the marsh and lake country between the post and the Kuluene forest. By dint of sitting under trees till birds settled in them above, I managed to bring in three or four pigeons a day. These I plucked in open view, sitting on the bluff above the nearby river, Tuatuari.

After a week had passed, a young warrior from the Kamayura tribe, an old man from the Waura, and the chief of the Mehinaku had all paused to examine my gun on their journeys to and from the post. It was a single-barrelled B.S.A. 12-bore and was impressively bigger than the .20 bore and .24 bores that were occasionally given out by Orlando as special rewards. The Indians had been impressed. Such a big gun for such little birds. Perhaps the civilizado was up to something.

Finally, on a morning when I had only brought in two birds, I looked up from my plucking to see Kaluana of the Aweti tribe standing above me. He was not big for an Indian, nor thick and stocky like some of the tribal wrestlers, but he gave the impression of being amazingly supple and well-built. His age was probably twenty.

"It's a nice pigeon," he observed encouragingly. He picked it up and absent-mindedly pulled the head away from the neck with a soft plop. There followed a meditative pause. "Tomorrow," he offered, "tomorrow I will carry you over to the forest by the River Kuluene. There are bush turkey there, and deer and pigeon, too." His face, grave and reflective, was turned sideways to mine and as I considered the unexpected altruism of this offer, I was disturbed by something unusual in the Indian's appearance. Then, suddenly, I noticed. The normal red, white, and black toucan feather ear-rings that project on a diagonal slant across the cheekbones of a warrior, were no longer hanging from his ears.

"There are toucan in the forest," I suggested casually.

Yes. It appeared there were many fine toucan by the Kuluene.

It was then agreed that Kaluana should call me "when the chicken first sings," and at about four o'clock next morning he must have slipped his hand through the hut's log walls to shake the rope of my hammock. Whang! There was a cry of anguish from the night outside.

Some days before, a passing and friendly Indian had brought a stork to join the two bush turkey, the two jungle fowl, the woodpecker, the parrot, the macaw, and the other animals which lived as we did in the Vasconcelos hut, pecking food from our plates, perching on our shoulders, and occasionally spattering thoughtlessly on to our hair. But the stork had not taken easily to the change. For the whole of two days it had not moved, standing a foot away from the edge of my hammock huddled up in itself at the end of long bare legs. A red patch of disapproval had developed at the end of its beak; occasionally it would sneeze and sneeze. The last straw—obviously—had been Kaluana's visit in the night. His furtive hand was a perfect target and the stork had attacked. There was a muffled cry from beyond the logs, and I awoke to the bird's hissing and beating wings.

Outside, I found the Aweti warrior sucking blood philosophically from the end of his knuckles. "The stork is savage," he muttered casually, and in a few minutes we were down by the river swimming our guns and clothes across. It was dark, without a moon, and we marched for two hours depending on the Indian's knowledge of the country. When the dawn arrived we were in the deep forest of the swamp territory by the Kuluene River. Kaluana weaved amongst the trees and tangles of scrub; I stumbled behind. Huge tree trunks soared into the sky above and mysterious alleyways and false paths led off through the brush and saplings on either side. It was the confusion of a nightmare, and I thought of the many occasions I had imagined with pleasure this moment of first entry into the forest of Xingu. I had always pictured a tall rampart of trees and then myself as the leader of a brave little group that would slip between the portals of two gnarled trunks into the jungle within. The Indians would point out orchids, creepers, and bushes. They would describe the trees and show me the different types of medicinal roots and leaves. And thus, from the general to the particular, a graphic picture would grow in my mind and I would feel master of the situation. Instead we had entered blindly in the night, and now there was such a mass of detail that it completely overwhelmed the civilizado's untrained senses. The vegetation concealed the forest as effectively as a fog hides the buildings of a London road. I clung to Kaluana as my only clue in a baffling wilderness.

Another hour and we stopped beneath a tall tree.

"Toucan tree," the Indian gleamed, and sitting down he made a shrieking noise by blowing through two leaves pressed tightly between his thumbs. He repeated this once or twice, and soon three birds arrived in the tree above.

"Cannon," Kaluana hissed, pointing urgently at my 12-bore. Then to elucidate the point in the gloating tones of massacre: "Slaughter toucan dead."

From my ambush, the tummied waistcoats of the friendly creatures above seemed uncannily like those of three gaitered bishops nodding kindly at each other in a London club.

"Good to eat," Kaluana insisted. Then with further inducement to my hovering indecision: "Good for feathers, too."

I lifted the gun to my shoulder.

"Boom!" Kaluana's face registered the explosion.

"Whoosh." Three disgruntled toucan took themselves off to another part of the forest. My first lesson in hunting had ended in failure.

But later in the day, Kaluana repeated his whistle—it seemed to make the birds curious—and I shot a toucan very high in a tall tree. It came whistling down all black and red and pompous, a sad little figure to be plundered by the lithe Indian at my side. He wrapped the feathers in a leaf and gave them to me; naked, he had no pockets. And then came a bewildering hunt, in which he snatched my gun and disappeared at great speed between the undergrowth; he killed a bush turkey. That was for the post. The toucan was for him. Our bargain was complete, and I had acquired an Indian who would teach me to hunt. It seemed that I had a redoubtable "cannon" and like every beast of burden would have to be trained to carry and manoeuvre it.

For a fortnight we went out on alternate days, each trip lasting without rest from four in the morning till two to four in the afternoon. Usually—with much protest from the "pack animal" part of the team—there was no food or water from the time of dinner at six o'clock the evening before, till our return twenty to twenty-two hours later. Then there would be a day rest. But in the second afternoon, Kaluana would call me, furtively, out into the clearing where no one could hear. (Every Indian arrangement is conceived in a melodrama of conspiracy.) Companionably, the Aweti would go through my pockets to see if anything new was to be examined, and afterwards the details of the hunt would come out.

The days passed. I began to learn something of the forest.

At first, that dark line of vegetation was approached with a certain amount of awe. This was part of the greatest forest on earth; writers had called it the Green Hell or the enemy of mankind. Outside, the swamp grass would be warm and cheerful, but inside the jungle seemed to contain all the horrors of a witches' wood. Nervously I would slip between the writhing shapes of twisted trees and enter a dark world where light, filtering through the leaves, would make the glades strangely eerie and mysterious. The shadows would play tricks before my eyes, the branches would rustle, small animals would creep away. My hands recoiled from the reaching tendrils of poison-bearing lianas, and the gun would swing nervously as snakes and pumas pounced from imaginary ambush. But soon the Indian's attitude began to overwhelm that of the civilizado. The forest became simply the environment of our lives. As a city dweller never looks at bricks, so the Indian never looks at a tree. There are saplings for making bows, and Jatoba for making canoes, and certain branches where animals like to sit, but there are never trees noticeable for self-conscious reasons—beauty, terror, wonder. The forest is their livelihood, and the eye of a travel writer would, for them, be meaningless.

On the other hand, the Indian's viewpoint is more accurate than that of a more imaginative man from the towns. He knows, for example, that in the jungle things go up and down, that they do not go along. Self-centred beings, we civilizados tend to assume that all life proceeds on the same plane as our own, that of the horizontal, whereas in the forest most life struggles up towards the sun and at death drops away from it. It is the rhythm of living. Trees battle with each other to gain their porthole on the sky, creepers wind their way to the top, then drop shoots to the ground, and finally send another struggling arm towards the sun again. Victory is the death of an arboreal giant. After standing rotten for many years, it comes crashing to the ground where the human level of earth is no more than a graveyard. The forest is, in essence, the trees that grow in it, and not, as we assume, the ground which holds them at their roots. It would be more accurate to conceive of the jungle animals as living in skyscrapers rather than on a piece of bush-covered soil. Different types of food are to be found at different levels in the vegetation strata, and so the animals live and feed and hunt in a movement that is upwards and downwards: not only the birds, the bees and flying insects, but also the anacondas, tiger cats, and ants. In the forest, the Indian thinks vertically.

In a similar way, if a city man describes a tapir or panther, he tries to portray it from what he has seen in the zoo. But not so the Indian of Xingu. When asked, he invariably imitates the animal's call. "That mummmm, muuummm," he would say for a puma. And soon I realized that in the forest where the range of vision could be limited to five yards, a hunt of hours would proceed without sight of the prey till that final moment when, camouflaged by branches and undergrowth, a bullet would be fired into something that was barely distinguishable as part of an animal. The jungle is a world of the ears. Because of this, the little I could remember from the zoo confused rather than helped, since imagination was determined to fit the sound to a suitable shape. Once I warned Kaluana that a puma was roaring in the bushes and was told that what I had heard was really the song of a frog. Later it seemed inconceivable that the creak of a breaking tree about to split in the wind was, in fact, an edible fowl, and that the screaming laugh of a hyena was merely the cry of a small pheasant-like bird. How strange that a soft honking should be the anger signal of a large anaconda, and that a roar as of two dragons challenging each other to battle across miles of jungle, was no more than the cry of a pack of small howler monkeys.

Little by little, however, Kaluana introduced me into this unseeing vertical world of the forest with its strange orchestra of Amazonian sounds. But at the last stage of every stalk he would seize my gun, whisper, "Stay here, Adriano," and finish off the kill for himself. The gun was for killing. I was its inevitable but deplorable method of transport.

After his fifth or sixth disappearance into the undergrowth at the keypoint in a lesson, I rebelled.

At his call on the next morning, I lay doggedly in my hammock. "I can't come," I whispered. "I am ill, Kaluana."

"What sort of illness?" he hissed suspiciously through the logs.

"It's difficult to explain. I am a foreigner. I don't know the Portuguese for it."

"Hmmm," said Kaluana from the darkness outside, where the cock had crowed once. He went off on his own, and later that afternoon I set out from the post on my first solo hunt. I canoed to a likely part of the forest and made camp as night came down.

. . . .

The moon was in the tree at the end of my hammock when I heard the faint whisper of sound. To begin with, I won-

dered if it was a mosquito buzzing nearby. I lifted my ears
above the cords of the hammock and listened, without moving, for five minutes.

It was roughly the hour before dawn. The sound came
very faintly again.

I leaned back and touched the cartridges in my shoes,
which were tied by their laces to the hammock rope behind
my head. On the ground, in what was the natural arc of a
falling hand, I felt the barrel of my gun resting on a broken
log. I had put it there on the previous evening when, on
reaching this bank of a darkening river, I had made these
few square yards the one point in the great waste of forest
that was significant for the presence of a being with brain
and purpose. Now the object of my purpose was making its
call.

A few puffs were enough to blow up the fire by my hammock, and a young carnival of flames lit the chewed bones
of a fowl that, Indian fashion, I had put on the fire the night
before; I could still remember the outside, strong with the
taste of burnt flesh, and the inside with the blood of raw
meat. The fire flickered across my gun, and while I was test-
ing the firing mechanism a centipede that had slept there
during the night crawled out and dropped to the ground.
Soon after, I began the hunt for my prey. The civilizado had
led himself to believe that he had learned from the Indians.
He slid into the forest feeling as lethal and catlike as a tiger.

There was just enough light from the moon and the false
dawn to etch shapes into the dark of the forest night and to
silhouette the faint depressions of the Indian trail. It was
surprisingly easy to follow. In the height of day, the jungle's
trellis-work of leaves tends to splash confused puddles of
light across the ground that camouflage rather than reveal a
path. Now, the little light that there was, made a sharp difference in tone between the trodden track and the unbeaten
surrounding ground. My feet followed it, feeling through

the soles of my gym shoes along the beaten line; if they strayed on to unbroken twigs or leaves, they automatically sought the path again.

I crept quietly, looking no further than my footsteps, and aware that strange things seemed to be peering at me from the darkness. I forced myself not to think about them. If the monsters of imagination stalk by one's side, it is hard not to look to left and right, and I had already learned that peering about in the forest made my eyes slow to see and react. The constant effort of focusing and refocusing between lianas a few inches from my nose, through a maze of tangled branches at varying distances to an object some hundred yards away, brought nothing else than a stabbing headache. It was better to walk "carelessly" like the Indian, with eyes specifically on the ground and generally everywhere, watching not for colour or shape, but registering in split-second attention any movement within an arc of 250 degrees. By not "looking" in front, the Indian seems to catch movement behind. And though at first I had attributed this to sixth sense, I later realized it was an instant reaction to something to which every part of his senses were tuned. Movement. It is betrayal in the forest.

With such limited vision, my ears were therefore the radar of the hunt. I tried to pause for a fraction of a second at the arc of every step to gain a moment of silence and listening above the crackle and noise of my own progress. When I had first seen an Indian listening with his mouth open, I had thought that concentration had relaxed the muscles in his face. Now, straining to hear, I too dropped my mouth down to avoid the faint rasp in the nose that is the sound of a passing breath.

There it was! Like the soft vibration of a distant outboard motor. It was the cry of my victim. Not a sharp sound tied to a specific point in the forest, but a vague purr on the air that had to be located with the slow turning of my head, careful to avoid the creak of a neck vertebra that would distort and confuse the trembling on my eardrums.

The air quivered once again. It was the summons of male to mate. I left the Indian path and pursued the line of the call.

The forest in this part was close to the river, and I was able to walk quietly on the tracks of a tapir's route to water before diverting on to the sodden ground of a stream-bed. This led in the direction of the summons, and as I knew my beast would probably be sitting high in a tree above a shallow mere, I hoped that the watercourse with its chance of quiet movement would lead me to him. Slowly and cautiously I walked, trying to imitate Kaluana's tread, so balanced that when his foot descended on a twig he was able to pause in movement and divert it to another place. Silence was vital. This part of the forest was hunted often, and my adversary would be listening and watching. At the faintest suspicion his cry would cease and I should be quite helpless in the maze of jungle—a navigator lost without a guiding beam.

By good luck, a breeze was blowing into my face and I moved forward in spasms, waiting till each gust shook the leaves in a covering "smokescreen" of sound. By now the call had swelled into a rich snore, and the crucial stage was at hand. He must be less than a hundred yards away.

In front was a tiny mere, silver in a moonlight that was combining with the first brightening of day. I waded in. Twigs fell with the breeze and set up ripples in the water. Fish occasionally leaped with a splash so that the faint signs of my progress did not disturb the creature above. Small trees put up an umbrella of protection over my head; gaseous muds sent up bubbles of decay under my feet. I climbed on to a giant tree trunk that had fallen into the deep part of the pool and crept along it with three cartridges dry in my mouth. And then, once again, back into the fetid, stirring swamp.

By this time the snore was close above, a rich purring sound like an uncle snoozing after dinner. I knew that my victim would be sitting at least thirty yards up in one of Amazonia's giant trees and that I should have to be almost underneath before the range was short enough to fire. Even then, I should be forced to creep in the undergrowth to find both a clear tunnel for the shot and an angle that would expose the head or breast. Step by step I advanced, making such an effort to be quiet that my legs grew stiff and my joints began to creak. In their effort to hear, my ears almost seemed to curve forward as they strained at the tangled criss-cross of branches above. At the first suspicion the call would cease, and I would have to crouch without a glance or upward movement of my head till it started once more. If seriously alarmed, the snorer would cry. First a jump on to his legs, then a startled danger signal, which, being a shriller sound, would be easier to pinpoint. Then another signal, and a second step, and he would take the plunge into space. I would have about two and a half seconds between alarm and departure.

His life depended on seeing the hunter. My kill, and the post's dinner meant several seconds of foresight, so that I could manœuvre and work my barrel up slowly between the branches. There is no possibility of "swing" in the forest.

Now I stood in the water, peering through a trellis-work of leaves. I quartered the tree in front and ruled out the camouflaged places where he could not possibly be. The moon was still up, but the first rays, as the sun pulled itself over the rampart of the earth, were beginning to strike at the tops of the trees. If his mistress did not answer before

the sun, the demands of breakfast would send the caller elsewhere.

And then I saw something. It was no more than a stir of
a leaf, but a stir that occurred with every snore. I moved
slowly behind my screen of foliage. I peered about for a clear
tunnel through the branches till I saw the leaf again from
another angle, and beyond the leaf a tail, and beyond the
tail a great Roman Emperor of a bird. A Cæsar's beak it had,
crimson against a head of purple, and a breast that was
brown and gold and bigger than a swan's. It was the mutum
castanho, the largest of the bush turkeys. Flying, he would
look as big as a goose. Walking, he makes as much noise on
dry leaves as a marching man. The wing-span varies from
four to six feet.

Slowly I eased the gun between the twigs and branches
and started to tip the muzzle cautiously up towards the sky.
Suddenly his cry sprang out sharp as a soccer whistle. It
ended in a long drawn-out hiss. He had seen. One jump and
the mutum's back was towards me. As the stock came to my
shoulder, he bent his legs for the leap. One more hiss, and
then I caught him smack in the tail and slightly to one side.
Triumph!

Thirty to forty yards above the ground the perch had
been, and so dinner hit the deck with a thud. And then, to
my horror, dinner leaped to its feet and started racing off
through the undergrowth. Complete humiliation!

With a most un-Indian howl, I tore after what should
have been my first solo kill and what now appeared to be
just another failure. A shot in the rump at that range would
no more than wound. I plunged and tore and writhed
amongst the undergrowth. The mutum was ahead, running
with a strange rolling gait that was both dignified and un-
dignified, like Henry VIII behind a reluctant mistress. He

was slower than I was, but then branches, lianas, and thorns were not tearing the shirt and skin from his back. After sixty seconds I realized that he was drawing away, but suddenly another mere in front forced him to turn and run at right angles along the bank. Cutting across the triangle, I soared through the air and came down upon him. Smack. In a great welter of mud, water, dead leaves, and feathers, we thrashed about until the hunt came to its end. I was as cut and torn as if a puma had been my quarry.

But five minutes later, a fifteen-twenty pound meal was swinging tied to a liana five feet above the ground with a twisted network of twigs to act as camouflage against hawks. Proudly I slipped another cartridge into the breech and went looking for the mate. The bush turkey is the easiest prey in the forest and the bread and butter of man armed with a gun. It was my first lesson from the Indians, but also the most important. Even if I learned nothing else, I was now self-sufficient in the jungle of Xingu.

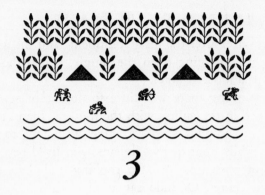

3

ORLANDO'S CUIABA

IT WAS LATE in the afternoon when I returned to Capitao Vasconcelos with my first kill tied to the gun across my shoulders. The mutum hung black and purple with its long wings almost trailing on the ground, and two jungle fowl —shot on the way home—swung from the other side of the barrel. Their feathers, red and brown, waved like victory flags on the mast of a pirate ship.

As I climbed up the steep bluff to the post, half a dozen Indians whooped and yipped in the traditional greeting for a returning hunter. Clearly, they were hungry. I left the fowls in the security of the kitchen and then went down to the little river, Tuatuari, that flows shaded by trees to one side of the Vasconcelos clearing. There a log had been cut for a seat, the water looked as bright and sparkling as crystal, and the sand was clear enough to use as soap. I swam and afterwards lay in my hammock as the evening sun filtered through the hut's log walls and trickled across the sand that had been spread across the floor. Perhaps Vasconcelos had seemed a hovel after the disappointment with the aeroplane but now on emerging from the jungle, it had the air and comfort of a modern hotel.

Next morning there was little to do except sew up the clothes torn in the gallop with the mutum. Juan once went out to the "hospital shed" to give medicines to visiting warriors, whilst four or five Indians who lived permanently in the hut passed to and fro cooking and doing various household chores. Orlando sat at his end of the building talking to some visitors who had come in from a tribe eighty miles away.

In this southern part of Xingu only a single wild tribe remains, and the other eight are so blended that they jointly form a group known as Xinguanos. Vasconcelos, or "Orlando's Cuiaba" as they call it, is their meeting-place. On this morning, fresh visitors had just come in. Tribal gossip was passing to and fro, and Orlando listened and joked and told the news from the other tribes. Otherwise, the place was strangely quiet for a post that was the capital of a land the size of the British Isles. At Indian stations elsewhere in Brazil one saw missionaries teaching in schools, preaching in churches, and showing the Indians how to improve the economics of their livelihood by modern techniques and tools. Here Orlando just sat muttering over gossip and tribal legend. Schools and religion, he had said a few days before, could be as destructive to the Indian as the bullets of pioneers. The chasm between the civilizado and primitive mind was so great that what seemed the benefits of civilization to us were in many cases the tools of destruction for the Indian.

An hour or two later, the visiting tribesmen left and a little boy named Claudio in honour of Orlando's brother, came into the room. He had ugly features, very thick-set and squat in the fashion of his Sherente parents, but he was a

great favourite of Orlando. He tried to swing on his hammock. Orlando rustled mysteriously in his pocket.

"Claudio wouldn't like a sweet from the old man's pocket,
would he?"

Claudio said he would.

"Claudio can't have a sweet until he has told the old man
where the Sherentes live.

"The Sherentes live over there." Orlando pointed in the
wrong direction.

"No, they live over there." Claudio knew the game and
pointed to the east.

"No. You don't know where the Sherentes live. You are
not one of the strong Sherente tribe. I have found you out.
You are a weak Karaja."

Claudio's father was a "civilized" Sherente from the State
of Goiaz who had come to work at the post. To be called a
Karaja was an insult.

"I am not a Karaja." Claudio stamped his foot. "I am a
Sherente, Sherente, Sherente."

"Do you love the old man?"

Claudio said he did. He got his sweet and went away.

"You pay too much attention to that boy," Juan spoke
from the other side of the hut. "You'll spoil him. In fact,"
the words assumed the tone of considered opinion, "you've
spoiled him already."

Orlando made no reply. He lay back in his hammock—a
somewhat incongruous figure, with the post's tame macaw
grumbling on his shoulder. Perhaps he was the ruler of this
great land of Xingu. But it was difficult to see how or why.

"Adriano," his voice came lazily from the other side of
the hut, "how did your hunt go yesterday."

I got up and went to sit beside him. I related the details
of the hunt and then asked about the Indians who had come

in that day. Orlando replied, and gradually in the placid mid-day calm of the post a conversation developed, wandering idly from subject to subject till it rested finally at the Fawcett story.

The subject came up because some weeks before, I had met an Indian with two arm bracelets joined by a band across his chest. He had introduced himself as one of the Kalapalo tribe, and I had complimented him on his Portuguese. I told him that I was "Ingleze" and he told me that some Englishmen like me once visited his village.

"Were they three men a long time ago?" I had asked.

"Yes. Before I was born." (He was about twenty.) "One was old."

"He had two companions?"

"Yes, tall."

"Young as I am?"

"Yes."

"How did they come?"

"They came," he said, "by walk. Then they slept. And then they went by canoe. And then they walked."

"Are they dead?"

"Yes," he said. "By the lake."

Even at the beginning of this conversation with the Indian I had suspected that I was talking to one of the tribe who are said to have murdered Colonel Fawcett, one of his sons, and his son's friend, Raleigh Rimmel, thirty-three years before. I refrained from asking how they had died.

"Does Orlando Villas Boas call him Fawcett?" I inquired.

"No," was the reply. "Forcetti."

A few days later I had heard the whole story from Orlando himself, but as it is one of the most fascinating mysteries of the jungle, we went over it again. I said that people in England still wondered what had happened to the explorer who had disappeared whilst looking for the lost cities of Atlantis

in Xingu, and I asked him to repeat the story for me again
as accurately as he could.

Orlando swung in his hammock. He told me that little
had been discovered in the past about the Colonel's fate
because no one had been able to live with the Indians long
enough to inquire with caution.

"When I first came here twelve years ago, all the tribes of
the Xingu knew that the Kalapalo tribe had killed the three
Inglezes. But I had to live with them for a year before they
showed me the grave.

"At that time, Adriano, Izerari was chief, and he said
that he would show me the grave when the rains were over.
But he died before that, and the next chief, Yacuma, was
frightened. I did not mention the subject and he died. Then
I talked to Comatzi, who wasn't a chief then, and he showed
me."

Orlando's face was reflective as he talked, and he seemed
to be going through the points deliberately one by one.

"All the Kalapalos came to the top of the cliff by the lake
and sat in a semi-circle. They made me promise that no
aeroplanes would come and after that they told me how the
killing was done.

"At the end of three hours Comatzi pointed to a mound
close by my feet. 'That is the grave,' he said. 'It is too small,'
I replied; 'Englishmen are big men.' But Comatzi drew a U
in the ground and said he was buried like that—doubled up.
'That's the head,' he said. And I dug and found that it was."

I then asked Orlando for the Indian's story of what happened, and he went on to tell it to me very much in the
language and style of the Indians themselves.

. . . .

"The three Caraiba were one old and two young. They
carried things on their backs, had guns, and one was lame.

They came from the west with Aloique, chief of the Naku-kuas, and his son, who brought them from their own village on the Kuliseu River.

"At that time, all the Kalapalos were in their fishing village to the east beyond the River Kuluene, except for Kavuquire and his son, who were in the main village. These two agreed to guide the Inglezes to the fishing settlement, so that they could pass beyond, into the country to the east.

"Next day they set out at dawn—two Nakukuas, two Kalapalos, and three Inglezes. After travelling for a day and a half the old man of the Inglezes spoke roughly to Kavu-quire, blaming him for saying that the journey would only take from the rise of the sun to the sun's height. He was fifty-eight and the heat is great.

"Later the old man, whom the Indians took to be chief, shot a duck and Kavuquire ran to pick it up, fingering and looking until it was snatched from him as if he had been about to steal. Then, when they arrived at the small lagoon by the Kuluene, the chief of the Inglezes spoke harshly again, because the canoe Kavuquire had promised had been taken to the other side.

"By this time Kavuquire was angry. But he had heard the rattle of collar (beads) in the Inglezes' packs and so kept silent, thinking in his head that he would get a reward; this is the Indian custom. When they reached the village he was given nothing, but kept silent again, hoping that they would make presents at farewell on the following day.

"During the night the Colonel cut up his duck with a knife, and when a boy played with the handle, he brushed his arm roughly aside. ['If you don't know how serious that is,' Orlando said, 'hit one of the male children in the Aweti hut. The parents won't kill you because you are in Vascon-celos, but they will never speak to you again.']

"Next day the village gathered to say good-bye on the bank of the little lagoon. No presents were given.

"Kavuquire demanded death. Caiabi, the chief, agreed. He was a cautious man and said it must be beyond the lagoon where the Nahukuas would not see.

"While Kavuquire, Kuluele, and one other ran round to lay ambush, the boy, Tuendi, paddled the Inglezes across. At the other side there was a cliff, small but sheer, and the chief of the Inglezes climbed to the top first, leaving the two others to bring up the baggage.

"As he got to his feet, he turned to look down on the young men below. Kavuquire came out from behind his tree with a club he had cut from a sapling. He struck his blow on the back of the neck. The old one cried, wheeled, clutched a tree and started to fall swivelling round it. Kavuquire hit again on the right shoulder, and the body collapsed, doubled up on the ground.

"At the cry, the young Inglezes dropped their baggage and started to climb the cliff. Immediately, the two Kalapalos hidden in the bushes at the bottom leaped out and struck up at their necks and heads. The bodies toppled back into the water.

"When Kavuquire, Kuluele, and the others returned to the village, Caiabi said they must bury the bodies. He was a cautious man and was frightened that the Nahukuas would tell Indians who were friends with the civilizados.

"Caiabi talked to Kavuquire on the first day, and he did nothing; he talked to him on the second day and he did nothing; but on the third day he went with some others. Putting leaves into their nostrils, they scraped a shallow hole by the old man. Then they lifted his feet, and then his head so that he lay nearly as he fell. They took everything from the body except for the machete clutched in his hand. ['Indians don't like touching the dead, and even throw away a club after use,' said Orlando. 'The machete has been traced to a German firm who sold all that particular stock in England during the 1920's.']

"The young ones," he concluded, "were still below, swollen in the water. So they were towed by a canoe and left in the centre of the lake. Then, from fear, their equipment and clothing were thrown into the Kuluene."

After he had finished, I asked Orlando about a solution to the Fawcett mystery. On a previous visit to Rio to collect equipment for the Xingu journey, I had been told by a Brazilian anthropologist that the bones sent out by Orlando were much too small to be those of Colonel Fawcett. On the other hand, Orlando told me that almost all the reliable authorities on the Mato Grosso agreed with the verdict originally given by Commander Dyott, the leader of the official 1928 rescue expedition. He had been taken by one of Fawcett's guides to the village of the Nahukuas and there had found Fawcett's trunk. The chief in the village had then told him that the three explorers had marched over to the Kalapalos only one and a half days away, and though Dyott had been unable to follow this clue himself, Orlando's discovery seemed to complete the case. Except for one thing: the bones were smaller than those of the Colonel. It seemed as if an unbroken chain of evidence ended in a complete contradiction, and I suggested to Orlando that possibly the Indians could have told him the story but concealed the right bones elsewhere for reasons of fear or superstition. Orlando's answer was to shrug his shoulders. After his discovery of the Kalapalo grave, Colonel Fawcett's son had implied that Orlando invented the story for financial reasons, and since he was the only person connected with this highly profitable literary subject who had published nothing about it, he was naturally incensed. If anything more was to be done for the

Fawcett family it would have to be done by someone else. We were interrupted by lunch—rice with bush turkey. As I walked away, I felt that my interest in what had been said was not so much in the fate of Fawcett as in the way the telling of the story had led Orlando to depart from the mood in which he explained his work and policy to civilizado visitors. Words like "justice," the "good of the Indian," and "welfare" did not occur, and he seemed to have described it from the viewpoint of the Indian rather than through the eyes of a civilizado looking for another civilizado. This was, no doubt, a commentary on his methods and aims. Fawcett had come tramping through the wastes looking for a great goal; Orlando appeared to have drifted through the jungle with little purpose even though on an official assignment. Fawcett had slept a night with the Kalapalos before pushing further and further on; Orlando had dallied for a year, apparently because he liked the place. It was not the typical behaviour of an explorer, and I wondered if something in this unusual aspect of his character had appealed to the Indians. Fawcett had had some experience and yet, apparently, had made several mistakes in a few days. Orlando cannot have made many, for I had often known Kalapalos to canoe a hundred miles just to have a talk with him.

Later that afternoon, a bark canoe—not much more than a sheet of cardboard curled at the edges—came gliding through the Tuatuari's clear water and beached on the sand at the landing-place. A bronze figure rose to stand very graceful in balance on the bark that was floating feather-light on the water. He lifted out his hammock, his wife, his child, his pot. Then he walked gravely up the steep bluff to the hut.

I asked one of the Indians who lived permanently at the post what this man had come for.

"Oh, just to pass the time," he said. "Like us, he has time to pass." Or to put it another way, Indians don't have dirty stories in our sense, but when one has a story, he puts his wife in a canoe and goes to tell Orlando.

It was, I began to realize, upon this friendship and willingness to listen to the man at Vasconcelos that the "kingdom" of Xingu was founded. The ideas of command and punishment are incomprehensible to Indians; if any improvements were to be made, they would have to come through manipulation of personalities and tribal politics. Perhaps all Orlando's hours of idle conversation served some deeper purpose. Exactly what this was, I had not yet found out but it was probable that the usual missionary trilogy—religion, education, sanitation—was not amongst them. It seemed that the whole problem was analogous to my original attitude to the post of Capitao Vasconcelos. As I came from the aeroplane with the standards of civilization still predominant, the place had seemed a sordid pigsty without purpose. As I came from the jungle, it had had the beauty of an oasis in the wilderness. Perhaps Orlando was attempting something bigger and possibly more difficult than was at first apparent.

Mount Roraima: "The Lost World" of Conan Doyle

Orlando Villas Boas with an Aweti woman and Sherente child

The famous frontier of civilization, the River of Deaths

The main hut at Capitao Vasconcelos

The view across the marshland to the hunting country of the Kuluene Forest

Bebcuche pounding rice at the post

4

POISON FISHING

FOOD IS ALWAYS a problem at Vasconcelos and, one particularly hungry day, when it was still many hours till our next meal of rice and beans, I went to look in my kitbag. There, under the socks and packets of trade goods, were a pair of underwater flippers, a mask, and a cheap second-hand gun.

Fish!

As I walked down to the river I hoped that the Indians who were visiting the post from their surrounding villages would think that I had done this many times before. In a particularly tall tree by the shore, a Kamayura warrior with bent bow was waiting for a target. He was watching a river that was so clear that ten feet down it was possible to see streaks and flashes of silver. In the water, splashing, were two Mehinaku women whose supple backs had been painted red with the forest dye, urucu. I put on my flippers, mask, and breathing tube, and without a word to the Indians, who said not a word to me, I entered the water and floated downstream with the current.

Noise. I had always thought of the world of the underwater as something quiet, but now, every thirty to forty seconds, fishes in flight from this incredible battle of survival would erupt through the surface and crash down again in an exploding water-spout of spray. Under the surface, these shock waves were multiplied in force. The roar seemed like that of a depth charge.

I dived to the bottom and was surprised to discover that fallen trees still retained their leaves, creating twilight forests in the river. There, bigger fish, like the tucanare—fast and powerful as cruisers—awaited their prey. I hovered outside these dark caves of decaying vegetation, watching for two eyes or a faint flick of a tail that would reveal one of these monsters keeping its position against the current.

In the clear sandy part of the river where the Indians washed their pots, I noticed that the piranha, so much described by other travellers in Amazonia, were patrolling. These cannibal fish have a notorious and exaggerated reputation in the literature of Amazonia because, in towns like Cuiaba and Manaus, foreigners are taken, as a tourist attraction, to the stretch of river below the slaughter-house where blood-maddened piranha can literally strip a man or cow to its skeleton in a matter of a few score seconds. In other conditions and at other times they are dangerous too—for instance, at evening in the Kuluene River—but not to the extent of one writer's statement that "no one except a newcomer would be mad enough to bathe in a Brazilian river." This had led the quartermaster of my previous Oxford-Cambridge Expedition to equip every member of the team with thick rubber boots that reached to the thighs. After a year in the jungle, though I had watched many piranha with greedy, sabre-toothed mouths gobbling at refuse on the surface, I had never seen them attack anything living, ex-

cept fish caught on a line. These sometimes reached the
surface with the whole rear part of the body torn off. In this
little river the piranha looked no more than unthinking
robots patrolling up and down till the slightest disturbance
would draw the pack, as if sparked by an electric impulse.
Because of this incessant patrolling, few were ever shot by
an Indian arrow; but for a gun they should be easy prey. I
advanced cautiously. Their bodies from the side were as big
as soup plates, and, if approached through a smoke screen of
muddy water where Indians were bathing, a school would
pass broadside on within two or three feet of me. They were
almost as easy to hit as the sting rays, which bask in the mud
and sit so tight that only a few days before a careless boy had
been badly slashed when he stepped on one.

After this first, brief reconnaissance, I decided to spend
much of my time hunting underwater for the Vasconcelos
table. Fishes in thousands and in varieties that were infinite
seemed to swim in that small river. And not only fish. Lower
down there were turtles that would pop their heads out of
the water, beady eyes indignant at the noise of an outboard
motor; so close did they come that a diving Indian could
catch them by the leg. There were baby crocodiles that always seemed asleep but never were when you tried to swim
up on them, and a small eight-foot anaconda that swam
regularly in a pool not far from the post. Sometimes, looking up through the crystal of the water, I would see a land
snake crossing above, its body flailing, but its snout held like
a dog's, dry above the surface. And once I watched the rub-
bery motion of a black electric eel that an Indian shot in the
water not far from me. Every time the arrow was moved in
its wound, it sent off shocks—presumably via moisture in the
sand—to feet placed half a yard away. And I remembered
how the explorer Humboldt had once—as an experiment—
driven some horses into a pool. The eels had rubbed them-

selves up and down their bellies discharging electric shocks till, stunned and panting, the horses had drowned in less than five minutes.

Over the weeks I learned some of the habits of these water-living creatures. Where there was a commotion by the shore, there, like automata, would go the piranha; but a small brown fish called the piau would always sink to the bottom and hide under logs and in little caves. The tucanare would seldom explode out of his hiding-place except for a prey near the surface, and the sting ray always moved in darts, slowing down and then darting forward again. The anacondas appeared to keep permanently to the place, where they must have had a nest, and they resolutely ignored all my attempts to interest them in new forms of life. It is traditional for Amazonian travellers—who also happen to write books—to be ambushed by an anaconda when a friend chances to be passing by. This friend is invariably carrying a loaded camera that can only be used from such an angle that authentic background details cannot be included in a picture of a life and death struggle in which the friend makes no attempt to interfere. Orlando Villas Boas did tell me later, however, that anacondas are so much creatures of reflex that after a big one has digested its last prey it will emerge from its lair and strike at the first large-sized movement that passes by. This explained the two-day struggle he had once seen between an anaconda and a crocodile, indigestible and very difficult to kill. The two had moved up and down in the water for two days in an almost motionless combat of strength. Strangely quiet except for their groans, the anaconda tightened its thick coils, the crocodile tried to bite its way out. But the snake had so relaxed its body by the saurian's jaws that there was no easy surface to grip. If the king of the water, I felt, could be so stupid as to attack a crocodile, and was then so bound by reflex as not to let go, surely intelligent, hungry man, learning from observation and armed with a

gun—admittedly tinny, second hand and with a poor spring
—could kill an even more stupid little fish.

That was the theory. But for two weeks I tried; and day
after day I emerged empty handed to look at silent Indians
who had been equally silent when I had entered the water
two hours before.

But one night, when the Kamayura tribe had come for a
visit and their cooking fires were sparkling round the post,
I went to talk to Takuman, their chief. Preparations for
something were obviously afoot. The women were wrapping
mandioca pancakes in a sort of bamboo matting and the
men were squinting down their six-foot arrows and straight-
ening out the bends over the fire. Takuman was turning his
arrow-head reflectively amongst the embers. "Adriano," he
observed conversationally, "only plays like a child at fishing.
He thinks he's a fish and he isn't." He then was silent a little
longer, but finally offered to show me how to catch a fish
like Indians—and men—should.

A trap for poisoning had been built earlier that day.

An hour later, we went down to the water in the dark and
left behind us the chinks of candlelight that shone through
the logs of the Vasconcelos hut. As we moved away, the
post's phonograph sounded tinny in our immense, impassive
waste.

We landed where the bank was low and padded through
the night, a dozen of us in single file. We walked quietly,
occasionally shining my torch at a rustle in the forest, and
after half an hour reached more water and more hidden
canoes.

Two men in the front had paddles. Two men in the back,
as well. They paddled in hard bursts so that the canoe darted
over the water. Then they rested, paddles over knees, listening to see if the forest that stretched for several hundred
miles on either side would notice the canoes gently hissing by.

Once we drew into a bank. My torch flashed. A curved, lithe Indian form bent over the water, bow arching in hand. The arrow sped and then bobbed and danced in the water.

"Tucanare," Takuman whispered, and I heard a crunch as his teeth bit into the gills. Another flash. A second bobbing arrow, and a second fish. This time he spat gently to get the scales and living flesh out of his mouth. In five minutes we had enough to eat that night and continued our journey to the fish-trap, hurtling over the water, through dark tunnels of vegetation, across broad meres and down narrow reedy channels till two or three hours later the paddling stopped and an Indian whispered we must be very quiet. We were, and it was hardly possible to hear the canoe as it touched bottom, or to catch a sound from the silent forms that carried a fence of reed and branches across the opening to the trap. The gate was closed.

Immediately, everyone talked, slung hammocks from the trees, laughed, and lit a fire. The fish were caught in a shallow inlet the Kamayura had fenced off that morning, and now that the gate was closed we could hear them leaping behind the trap.

"Many fish," Takuman said. Just then we heard one land in the canoe that had been put on the outer side of the trap. Strong specimens leaping to freedom would bang and rattle in the canoes' curved sides till they had gasped out their life.

Dawn came as the Indians yipped and whistled long hollow sounds into the forest to welcome and echo the day's beginning. I found Takuman beating a bundle of sticks on a rock. The sticks were timbo, a green liana that can be gathered almost anywhere in the Amazon forest but that had now been dried brown as the arm that was pounding it. When the pulpy fibres were put into the water, a detergent-like foam was given off and Takuman leaped up and down, drumming the water with his legs. As the ripples and mud spread outwards, one could imagine the poison seeping through the mere like gas over a battlefield.

They beat the timbo for about an hour—eight men, each with several bundles. Then the fish began to leap—one every few seconds. About half cleared the canoes to freedom and about half landed to gasp themselves into extinction. My English soul pined at the inefficiency. When there were so many fish in the trap, why let them go when a higher fence would have been so easy to make? And then I noticed that it was only boys who were shooting at those fish that swam gasping to the surface preparatory to the leap. One little boy, only just old enough to hold a bow, was obviously putting no enthusiasm into his work, and the men started to shout at him, throwing sticks into the water at his feet. Takuman was standing by an older boy directing him to shoot here and there, and watching as the arrow leaped and squirmed when it struck a target or remained dead when it registered a miss. Weren't there bows and arrows lying nearby, and wasn't Takuman, to my certain knowledge, an excellent shot?

A few minutes later, when one of the fish that had been pulled off an arrow started to flop and bounce its way to the water, my question was answered. I put out my foot to stop it, and Takuman leaped over and hauled me back.

"Only boys," he said, "may hunt the fish." I later learned that this meant men without sexual knowledge.

For an hour we watched while two gull-like birds darted and screamed and a pair of king vultures soared above. That night, pumas would come out of the forest, and cat-like on the edge of the mere, paw for the remaining fish. But now the water was full of dark shadowy forms that would come floating to the surface, gasp with their mouths beating open and shut, and finally turn their white bellies to the blue sky, and die.

When the sun was an hour from its height, Takuman, as chief, entered the water, raised an arrow above his head, and stabbed a fish. As son of the dead chief he had thus initiated the long chain of fishings and feasts that would lead up to the Quarup, when, after a night of incessant dancing, the first ray of sun would herald the feast of Mavutsinim, the Indian Creator. Then the chief's soul would be present in the village and all would worship their god and feel their ancestors walking in the huts amongst them. Indians of the eight tribes of the Xingu group would collect at the Kamayura village for the greatest dancing and wrestling since the Quarup years before.

It was an auspicious moment when Takuman lifted his arrow and struck through the water at that half-dead, squirming lump of food.

The other men seemed to hold their breaths. But once the barbed head had struck, they poled canoes into the mere with their bows, harpooned the fish, and shook them into the bottom. It was unimpressive work, like that of a civic scavenger in a London park. Some hours later, the whole catch was strung on vines from the forest and the canoes pushed off.

That night at Vasconcelos, piau, piranha, tucanare, sting ray, bicuda, and three giant trirao lay smoking on long stick racks over the Kamayura fires. Cooked like this, the fish would keep for three days, till the feast when they would all be eaten.

Takuman avoided looking at my underwater fishing tackle.

"Have we caught many fish this day?" he asked.

"Many," I said. "Between five and seven hundred." To a man who could not count, these must have sounded fine, laudatory words.

Takuman took a fish off the fire and ate with pleasure.

5

THE LITTLE QUARUP

EARLY NEXT MORNING the Kamayura set off back to their village, and forty-eight hours later I followed them along a trail that lay across the airstrip and wound through an area of poor soil where the forest was low. The grass was a golden brown, the trees had silver bark, and the deer stood in the shade because the Indians never killed them. My journey was at dawn. I knew that ever since Takuman's return, the tribe had been preparing for the "invitation" feast of the Little Quarup.

As I walked, I remembered the first time I had travelled this path and how my guide, after two hours, had suddenly vanished at the entrance to the village. There, surrounded by a semi-circle of five huts very much the shape and size of haystacks, had been a large and empty square. On its verge I had stood like an untried gunman about to walk up a cow-town street. The Kamayura had killed civilizados in the past. With an embarrassed coughing noise, I plunged into the black interior of the first hut on my right.

As my eyes were getting used to the dark, a strange noise grew to a crescendo, and two naked savages burst half-bent under the shallow door. They straightened up in a flaring shock of all the coloured finery of the Urua dance. Then they stood absolutely still, bodies black as ebony, glistening under sweat, flesh hard as marble, faces like two Inca death-masks.

"Good day," I gulped, and then feeling this rather inadequate to the occasion, "Porikoh." It was my only word of Kamayura, and I hoped it meant, "Hullo, I'm friendly, and I hope you are too."

"Good day to you, too," one of the savages replied in excellent Portuguese. "How's Vasconcelos, and what are things like in Rio these days?" He put down his flute, and I sank weakly on to a small Indian bench. It was like hearing Shakespeare from an Eskimo at the North Pole.

This had been my first meeting with Takuman. I learned that, in the ten years since Orlando first came into the region, he had picked up Portuguese and had once been flown to hospital in Rio de Janeiro. He was the son of the dead chief, and as the best wrestler in the village and the man most capable of dealing with the foreigner, he eventually succeeded in the political struggle that led up to his chieftaincy. His combination of traditional skills with a familiarity of Caraiba ways was a mark of the tribe.

On this July morning of my second visit, the men were dotted about the village painting their bodies for wrestling. They sat and stood in a square about half the size of a soccer field and around it were gathered five huts, each of them large enough for a score of people. Their palm thatch was a dirty brown, the dust on the square lay beaten and yellow, and the forest that could be seen above and between the buildings was dull and uninteresting. But the men were putting the grey powder of cinders on to bronze mahogany skin and then marking it with the gay reds and blacks of

the forest dyes, urucu and jenipapo. Each man painted from
a little gourd with the first two fingers of his hand. In turns
they decorated each other, executing designs and blobs and
coloured portraits as fancy took them.

Then, almost at the moment of my arrival, a strange honking noise came from one of the huts and the men cried
"AAAiieeee" in surprise and pleasure. In the dark entrance
of the hut, two mysterious objects could be seen moving up
and down, appearing and disappearing like a snake's head
under a charmer's influence. With a hard stamp on the earth,
the dance began. First a bamboo flute ten feet long honked
like an anaconda, then a man bending double in the black
doorway suddenly snapped upright in a blaze of light, his
yellow head-dress of Arara feathers gorgeous in the sun,
his naked body red with urucu and dappled with the mark-
ings of a snake. Behind him, but with one arm on his shoulder, a woman followed each of his steps, wearing no clothes
or ornament besides a wisp of a straw tail; she had the blood
of ritual scratch marks running down the brown velvet of
her thighs. Afterwards came another flute played by another
man as magnificently dressed, but with a snake's tail hanging down his back; then finally another woman equipped
like the first. They danced their happy anaconda-like procession from one hut to another, visiting each house in the
village again and again.

The dance did not interrupt the men who were painting,
and after a welcoming calabash of some mandioca drink,
I was left to sit on a log and stare at the village—five huts,
a large square, and naked men and women passing to and
fro. It was like a ring of haystacks round a patch of baked
earth, and, except for a few guns and shirts, it would have
been difficult to tell that these people had been in contact
with civilizados for more than a decade. The Villas had been
deliberately careful and slow, to lessen the shock of civiliza-

tion. Only essential tools—and but a few of these—had been allowed to enter.

I turned my head and gazed out over the lake that could be seen between the huts on the northern side of the village. It was called Ipavu. Four hundred years before, the Kamayura had lived by what their legend describes as "a lake that was savage"—almost certainly the sea—and so had been struck by the first onslaught of Portuguese adventurers and pioneers. They, like many other coastal tribes, had fled into the forest. One of these groups, searching in its misery for the Indian paradise, Maran-im, had crossed the two thousand miles from the east coast of Brazil to Peru in nine years. But the Kamayura had had a slower and more bloody progress. They had fought with whites and with the Indians whose territory they crossed. From their stories, it seems that they had finally ricocheted off the Karaja lands by the Ilha do Bananal, come down a western tributary of the Araguaia, and crossed the watershed till they hit a feeder stream of the Xingu. Here their journey ended. They had reached the fortress of South America.

"We lived near the river," a Kamayura had explained to me, "and fought and fought with the Juruna tribe. Then we went to a place called Jacare and the Juruna came, too, and we fight and fight. So, at last, we go to Ipavu where we had four villages round the lake, but there was much disease and the Juruna came too. But this time we had ten .44's (Winchesters) and we killed ten of them and they haven't come again. But there was much disease until the Kamayura had only one village left, and we crossed the lake to this side because of the mosquitoes on the other."

Ipavu was their last retreat, from the civilizado and the Indian wars that his pressure brought.

On my first visit, when I had lived for some days in Takuman's hut, I found, down by the water, a tall tree on whose side was drawn in black forest dye a peculiar figure. After that I noticed two or three more of them in the forest and became curious about the significance of the drawing.

"Who is the man painted on the tree?" I asked.

"He is the man who discovered Ipavu."

"Do you paint other Kamayura?"

"No."

"Was this man then a chief?"

"No."

"Did he later become a chief or the father of many men?"

"No."

"What did he do then?"

"He discovered Ipavu."

The importance of that event can hardly be underestimated by anyone who has spent a day with the tribe.

"Ipavu," the Kamayura cry in the cold hour before dawn when dogs can be heard fighting for the warm earth of the night's dead fires. "Ipavu! Ipavu!" One can hear them going down to the lake, their cries getting further and further away until they suddenly give way to ecstatic yelps of sheer delight. No other sound of man that I have heard expresses so much pleasure and astonishment at one single miracle of nature. They have reached the water. Outside, the air is cold and the Indians' naked bodies are icy from sleeping uncovered in a fibre hammock, but at that time of the day Ipavu is warm, and the Kamayuras dash in and swim like porpoises out from the shore. After that they paddle their dug-out canoes as the mist yawns and stretches under the sun, their bodies gorgeously tinted in the colours of dawn. They slowly fade into the distance, remote standing figures on invisible canoe floors, some going to fish, some going to hunt, and some going to the mandioca plantations hidden by the forest, but all making the day's first delightful crossing of their own, wonderful lake.

During the hours that follow, Ipavu is the centre of their lives. Down by the shores the children play, and in its shallows the women smooth the water over their hips and down their long hair, and then come striding out in a line with fast jerking steps. "Good water," they say to the stranger. "Beautiful lake." And even at night, when the men sit on the logs in the village square making quiet talk and looking at the stars, there is, so far as I could discover, only one constellation for which the Kamayura have a name. "There, that's the fisherman," they say, pointing at the Great Dipper which in this part of the world bends its rod-like shape over the waters of their lake.

These memories of my first visit came rushing back into my mind when I guessed that Takuman was going to use this morning of the feast to broach the ominous subject of presents. He came up and sat beside me. I had, of course, he observed, remembered my friends and brought back presents from Rio. Presumably I had been waiting for a suitable moment to give them out.

I told him what I had brought.

"You have red combs with sparkling glass in them," Takuman approved reflectively.

"And mirrors and beads too," I added.

"You have long fishing line and hooks to go at the end," he ruminated. And then, without apparent logic or connection: "The Kamayura don't like Orlando any more."

"Why's that. He's the friend of the Indian."

"Orlando gives no more presents."

"Maybe he has none to give," I defended. "He works for the government a long way away in Rio de Janeiro and no aeroplanes have been for a long time."

"Orlando is rich," Takuman stated decisively. "He has trunks of guns and trousers and bright shirts sent by the government for us. And he gives them all to savage Indians. Not us."

"Orlando is the friend of the Indian," I side-stepped.

"Many Brazilians want to steal your land, and Orlando is fighting for you."

"We prefer the Americano Ricci," said Takuman firmly. Ricci had come to take anthropological film some years before. "When he came, he gave us many beads and hooks and line."

"Orlando is fighting for this," I said, fingering the square's dust in my hands.

"Ricci gave us this," said Takuman, touching the blue necklace round his waist.

Beads for land, then poverty, decay, and death. It was none of my business to meddle in the Indian problem, but I informed Takuman that it was an old, old story. I told him about the land-grabber and the North American Indian, about the Australians and the aborigine, and about the Boer and the bushman of South Africa. He wasn't very interested and said he would think about it. I changed the subject.

"Are the Kamayura coming back from the post of Xingu today?"

"Some of them," Takuman replied. The thought did not seem to please him.

"Why only some? All the Kamayura should be here at the feast of the Little Quarup. Why have they gone away, Takuman?"

"They go because the Caraiba [the Air Force personnel at the post of Xingu] give them beads and fishing lines and bullets to work for them."

"Then why don't you stop them?"

Takuman looked dark and said nothing more about what was, in fact, a serious split between the conservative and radical elements within the tribe. It was not only shaking the tribe's ceremonies and beliefs at their foundations, but it meant that the women and children whose men were away were largely deprived of the meat-and-fish part of their diet.

The last measles epidemic, which had carried off 114 Indians, had been the result of a visit of this sort.

"Hooka. Hooka. Hooka. Hooka." Suddenly the air was shaking with the deep grunts of men as they stamped round each other, pounding the ground with their feet. The wrestling had begun, and dark Indian bodies were heaving on the ground, red, yellow, and blue belts of cotton sparkling in the sun.

It was curious, I thought, how simple an Indian village looks on first arrival—a handful of palm huts, naked people, and a few very plain possessions. It would take longer to make an inventory of a single European room than of an entire Xinguano village. But once you have been there a little time, how complex and confusing the life can become, each action invested with a significance deep and tortuous. Why, for instance, should a girl in the hut of Takuman be concealed from the light of the sun for the period of a year? Why could hunters not kill deer, and why only old men eat the flesh of the black monkey? That man before me had two wives who were sisters, and that woman over there could not take a husband till after the Quarup. Why? How could a primitive people who must have relied on taste alone, have learned that the deadly poisonous root of the mandioca when scraped, then grated, then washed ten times, dried and then cooked, was in fact an edible food? And why had the same ingenious mandioca discoverers not learned to weave the cotton they grew for their wrestling belts into blankets to keep out the cold at night? And so on, deeper and deeper into great labyrinths of Indian custom and prejudice.

The first time I had seen the wrestling, a huge and burly warrior of the Kalapalo tribe had been led from the door of the chief's hut to the centre of the village square. He was painted and stood lowering by the wrestling place—a bull in a taunting ring, one animal against a mob, but conscious of

its prowess and determined to slaughter. He remained quite
still and without movement for two minutes. Then a Kamayura stepped out and, with a loose movement of his hand,
scooped dust from close by the Kalapalo's feet; the other
scooped too. The challenge was accepted. Battle sounds rose
into the air; hard feet beat the ground; agonizing grunts
burst from two heaving chests. But, in fact, the fight was a
poor one and an easy victory for the Kamayura. The Kalapalo was allowed a minute to breathe and then another
Kamayura took him to a swift defeat. As man after man
came out, the Kalapalo became weaker and weaker, breath
gasping, head bent under the sun in a hostile village square.
Eventually he refused a challenge, then a second, then a
third, and the Kamayura "Druid" stood out in the centre and
taunted him in a high sing-song voice. The man had been
humbled in the dust, but no blood had been shed and the
hospitality of the village was his.

Amongst the Xinguanos, wrestling had become a means
of transferring rivalry between tribes into a bloodless expression, and this day, in the first big feast leading up to the
Quarup, it was to have another significance. The chief of
the Mehinaku tribe had arrived in the village an hour before,
gorgeous with a head-band of yellow Arara feathers and
followed by women loaded with blue and white beads set
off by the red of their paint. Now he engaged in "soft wrestling" to demonstrate the friendship between his tribe and
the tribe of Takuman. The dead chief who had expired a
year before had been a Kamayura, but his wife had been a
Mehinaku, and so the two tribes were to be the hosts of the
Quarup together. They would provide the food and they
would compete against the others.

After the wrestling, six piles of fish were laid on six mats
of basketwork under the supervision of a warrior who was
lord of the Quarup and all the ceremonies that were to lead

up to it. The food came from the house of Takuman and in the centre of the square the old Druid chanted a wailing song, head bent under the sky, stick beating dust off the earth.

"Take notice, all you people. Take notice of the hospitality that the Kamayura will provide. Tucanare, sting ray, and piranha well preserved over a smoking fire. The best bread from the mandioca. And look. Look, the women are even now cracking pequi nuts into the baskets."

Fish and bread were then laid before the Mehinaku chief; he drank from a calabash of mandioca liquid; his tribe was thereby invited.

An old man and woman who belonged to the Waura village were offered similar food and drink. Their tribe was to come too.

Then the lord of the Quarup shouted. "What man is travelling to the Kalapalos? Whose hunting will take him to the Kuikuros? What warrior will go to the Yawalapiti," and so on, till runners were arranged for all the tribes of the Xinguano group. They would have to travel fast without food or drink, and without equipment or clothes, till they came hot-foot to the village of their destination. Then they would sit in the sun till the chief returned from hunting. He would ignore them. He would eat. Finally he would walk out for a quiet talk in which the invitation would be delivered.

The feast of the Little Quarup would then be followed by a series of fishings at Morena where the rivers Ronuro, Batovi, and Kuluene join to form the Xingu. Here the sun, brother of the moon and child of the puma had created Indians. He had cut them, five women, from wild cane and breathed till they lived so that Morena was the place of creation. Then would come days of incessant dancing, and finally the tribes would flow in, gay with paint, wearing coloured belts, flaunting in the joyous aurora of their feathers. At sunrise on the day of the feast, the eight tribes of the Xingu would celebrate the coming of their creator, whilst the dead chief and all the souls that had died since the last Quarup would be present amongst them. Fires would be lit to keep the dead warm, food would be put out to satisfy their hunger, and no one could walk outside amongst the spirits at night. Then one soul would depart to the skies and the other to live amongst the people under the water— Xinguanos have two souls, one in the eyes and one in the ears. And afterwards the widows would clean themselves, paint on urucu, and accept the suit of other men. By this ceremony the Indians would have released their dead and expressed their understanding of creation and the universe.

What made the Little Quarup one of the significant moments in the year was the summoning of other tribes that had come to this hidden valley in the Amazon forest from every point of the compass. Few of them had any historical link of friendship, language, or culture. The Kuikuro spoke Karib; the Aweti, Tupi; the Waura, Aruak; and the Trumai came from an unclassified linguistic group. The Mehinaku were from the south near Cuiaba. There is evidence that the Kalapalos lived on the River of Deaths in the eighteenth century. The Kamayura came from the east. The instinct of many Indians is to kill strangers on sight, and these particular eight tribes had at first fought for scores of years. But gradually a strange peace had materialized, bringing with it a homogeneous culture. By the time the Villas entered Xingu, all the tribes wore the same ear-rings, the same haircuts, and used similar paints and dyes. Their foods were the same, their huts were all as if they were haystacks, their canoes felt equally fragile. Above all, the feast of Quarup had become the social expression of the entire group.

As the ceremony of the Little Quarup continued it became clear even to a stranger like myself that if this unity should ever be broken and this feast destroyed, the effect on the Indians would be many times more serious than the simultaneous English abolition of Monarchy, Parliament, Divine Worship, and the Cup Final. It seemed ironic that such an important and detailed structure of ceremonial living could have originated with a single article of trade.

I had once asked Orlando Villas Boas about the Xingu alliance—there are only one or two similar culture groups in Brazil—and he told me that his brother Claudio had a theory based on the Waura pot. Amongst the eight tribes, only the Waura, two days to the west, had the secret of earthenware. Without pots, mandioca bread and many of the Indian's meat and fish dishes could not be made; the pot, alone of the Indian's many possessions, was unobtainable from the forest. Earthenware was almost synonymous with wealth in the Xinguano community, and as each tribe had entered the area, it had tried to develop this trade with the Waura, who had become extremely influential in the land, acting as mediating diplomats throughout Xingu. Before the arrival of the Villas, the last of their pacifications had brought the Trumai under their protection, halted the Kamayura war against them, and drawn this last of the eight tribes into the group. The pot was the corner-stone upon which the Xinguano civilization was built.

As the sun began to drop, I went up to Takuman to say good-bye.

"Your presents," he said meditatively, "in your presents, did you bring any pans? Now," he added, "we need a new pan for our cooking."

I asked if Takuman did not have a Waura pot of his own.

"Yes, the Kamayura have Waura pots. But the Caraiba ones are better. They do not break. When we all have Caraiba pots, we will need Waura ones no more."

As I walked back in the cool of the forest, the sad logic of his words could not have seemed clearer.

6

KALUANA

HUNTING IS THE breath of life to an Indian. It passes unnoticed in the course of daily existence but only ceases in time of war or sickness.

During the days that led up to the Little Quarup I had resumed hunting with the Aweti warrior, Kaluana, and from that time a curious partnership grew up between us that was to last till I left Vasconcelos. For two or three days on end we would go out with no more baggage than salt, two hammocks, and a box of matches. We lived like nomads, free in the jungle, sleeping where we stopped, exploring new lakes and woods, and given over to forgetfulness in the sheer lust of the chase. We tracked the path of pig for several hours on end, Kaluana pointing at the marks where pumas —hunters like ourselves—had stood, looked, and meditated upon the spoor. We fished in the rich waters of the Kuluene, hauling out a four-pound piranha every few minutes, or used a bow to shoot at tucanare lurking beneath the shadow of the bank. Sometimes we slaughtered six or seven mutum in chaotic hunts of swift movement and screaming panicking birds.

During this time Kaluana took care that his civilized "gun carrier" should become less of a liability in the forest. He taught me to listen for two macucu fowl whistling at each other in the undergrowth so that I could creep between, and, adding one more whistle to the conversation, draw both towards me. (I never succeeded.) He showed how difficult it was to chase a pack of monkeys swinging through the trees and told how an Indian would mark the direction of their passage, and, with a swift flanking movement to the front, shoot from ambush as they came towards him. Jacubim fowl almost always sat above water where the view was fine, preferring the worn patches of bank where giant otters liked to bask and sunbathe; and if the crested mutum was high in a tree and impossible to shoot, Kaluana would imitate the mating cry of the female. The male would whistle in excitement and in a few moments come with his black-and-white-shirted front, striding straight into our guns.

The weeks passed and our friendship developed. But life with hunting Indians is a cold, almost icy existence, and friendship is merely an alliance between two animals for the common purpose of food and protection. Warmth between men does not exist, and between modern and primitive man understanding also seemed almost impossible to achieve. For as the weeks passed, I became increasingly puzzled by my companion, Kaluana.

The Aweti warrior was an impressive figure. Xinguanos have a fine eye for proportion and unlike other Indians do not distort their bodies with discs forced into their lips, staves thrust through their nose, or blocks of wood tearing at the lobes of their ears. On Kaluana's shoulders and thighs there were deep scratch marks made with the teeth of a shark-like

fish called the pirara; but these had been drawn symmetrical
to the line and flow of his limbs. In his ears he wore six-inch
bamboo pins tipped with a bole of toucan feathers so that
when he turned there was a flash of colour in the forest's
drabness; these were as perfectly proportioned to his Indian
head as pendant ear-rings are to a Marie Antoinette coiffure.
Otherwise, he hunted without clothes or finery. The scratches
and ear-rings did no more than set off the hard lines of his
body.

Once when I went to the Aweti hut and saw Kaluana
painted up with a small feather band like a Roman laurel
leaf around his brow, I asked if he was going to a dance.

"No," had been the reply. "No, I am just beautiful."

And he had been right. It was a beauty. One of absolute
functionalism. Kaluana's face was even, with a straight nose,
but in his eyes there was none of the sad wisdom that could
be seen when meeting older members of his tribe. This front
part of his head was an instrument for four senses, enclosing
a machine for deduction, all balanced and smoothed into a
streamlined shape. There was no expression. He was only
five feet six inches tall, and smaller than most Xinguano
warriors. He did not have Takuman's wrestling shoulders
nor the untiring stockiness of the Mehinaku tribe. But every
part of him was in perfect balance to his purpose as a hunter.
His muscles as he walked were like those of a tiger-cat; his
speed in the forest, a challenge to my eyesight. At the faintest sound, Kaluana could check one leg in the air, an arm
half-way through a movement, the whole body frozen in the
act of transferring balance from one foot to another, and yet
in such perfect poise that the position could be held for minutes on end. He moved like a wraith that, having no sub-
stance, can disturb no obstacle, but in his case the secret was
a form so supple that it automatically shaped and reshaped
itself without conscious thought as it weaved between the

bushes. At the end of a day, when I would be cut and marked all over, he would emerge without a single scratch on his naked skin.

Gradually I realized that what at first had seemed the Indian's almost supernatural sight and hearing were the results of tuning to a certain wave-length and a known objective. A learner driver at first finds it impossible to assess the speed of an approaching car, no matter how long he stares, but after a year's practice he can make an accurate judgment at a glance. In the same way, when Kaluana had first made me look along his pointed arm at a hiding animal, I had found it difficult to see. But when my eye had become accustomed to its silhouette and I knew the limited number of places where it would be likely to sit, my vision had become nearly as quick as his. But never had I even approached his speed of decision and movement.

Once we had been fishing by a river, with our guns two yards behind, when two jacubim fowl landed in a tree above our heads. Almost before I had registered their arrival, Kaluana flashed up the bank, snatched a gun, shot a bird, and picked up the other gun. He caught the mate as it was taking off.

This adjustment to the needs of hunting extended even to his conversation. Vatacu, the old Waura who occasionally went out with me, would sometimes sit on a log. "Do you know what that tree is for?" he would ask. Then he would tell me in minute detail how an Indian would come, clear the ground about, cut the bark, fell the tree, and shape the result into a canoe. Sometimes he would pick up a certain type of soil. "This is earth for making pots," he would say. Sometimes he would stop by the larvae of a wasp's nest and describe how they should be cooked. "Pass over smoke. Then eat."

This sort of information, Kaluana never volunteered.

Once I asked him to repeat a toucan whistle for me to learn, but he refused; toucan whistles were for toucans. In all our time together he never ventured any forest information unless he was actually engaged with that particular stick or animal or cry or leaf and, during the whole of a day's hunt and camp at evening, probably no more than a score of sentences would pass between us. His talk was functional, like the rest of his being.

At three o'clock on one particular afternoon we arrived at a small stretch of river by the Kuluene. It was dirtier, broader, and more ominous than any British waterway, but it was something beautiful in the forest—a hundred yards across and one quarter of a mile up and down, without obstruction to the eye. It was a *view*. To the Indians it was also a *place,* though almost indistinguishable from any other part of the forest. The floor was earth; the furniture, trees and bushes; and yet any Xinguano warrior overhearing its description would know immediately where it was. For just beyond the bank a short spit made a good landing-place for canoes, and a hundred yards behind my back there was a dry watercourse that was easy walking for the first part of the journey to Vasconcelos. Though there was no mark of man, this was Clapham Junction in the forest.

I unsheathed my machete and started to clear the saplings whilst Kaluana took a branch and swept a small piece of ground till it was clean of leaves, centipedes, and scorpions. Two hammocks were then slung six feet apart on tree trunks that were neither rotten nor laced with the little tunnelled tracks of termites. Once I had tied Kaluana's hammock to a rotten tree, and when he had climbed in, forty yards of broken timber had rained down on him. But this time I chose with care and in ten minutes the hammocks were slung. This was home.

We used small wood so that the fire would quickly form

embers for the mutum I had just plucked and gutted. In the post it took three to four hours to stew one of these birds, but now Kaluana put it straight on to the coals so that in twenty minutes the outside was charred and the inside was still red with blood. We tore it to pieces. I smeared salt on the meat, putting my finger into a little store in my pocket. Kaluana ate it as it was. Xinguanos take salt rarely, but when they do, it has to be without food and only top-quality pure salt that they make for themselves.

It was an hour after halting, when the mutum had been ripped to the shreds on its bones, that I lowered myself into the water. A long tree reached out into the river so that we could crawl down it to a place where no scum or vegetation floated on the surface. Swimming was not wise in this part of the Kuluene where the piranha, according to the Indians, were particularly hungry and attracted by the slightest splashing; the technique was to hang on to a branch and float. Dry lips opened, and the sweat that had drained out during the day's hunt was made up in an unceasing flow of warm khaki-coloured liquid. The water looked like sewage; it tasted magnificent.

When I got back to hang my clothes on sticks by the fire and slap at the insects that were grazing on my body, Kaluana had made a trellis-work "table" of green taquari sticks. On it, six fowl and a score of silver fish had begun a slow roasting that would last throughout the night.

"Adriano, let us go fishing."

I objected that there were plenty of fish already on the fire.

"They are only piranha," was Kaluana's comment. "Now in the evening is the time to catch big fish. Pintado [12 to 30 lbs.] and Pirara [12 to 70 lbs.]. There is a boy sick in my hut who likes Pintado."

I was very tired that night and so I told Kaluana that I had important things to think about. This statement with its implication of weighty and ominous matters to be considered, always impressed him, and he moved thirty yards down the bank and built himself another blaze for light. During the next two hours, periods of silence would be suddenly interrupted by a tremendous splashing as he hauled a thirty-pounder ashore. It would grunt and groan across the dark spaces of the river as he beat it over the head. Three minutes of violent noise, then silence.

Meanwhile, I sat in my hammock staring at the other river-bank, where several storks were fishing. Nearby, a big hawk-like bird swooped and honked like an express train, and the water around about surged with fighting fish. It was rush hour in the forest, when the daylight animals were going home to sleep and the nocturnal ones were setting out to hunt. The trees, the land, and the river seemed to vibrate with movement and excitement. The only point of human significance in the blankness of the dark and the cruelty of this savage world was the little blaze of my fire. Occasionally, I heard the Aweti's thwacks and grunts. They were a lone sound that meant friend and ally.

Kaluana and I were, I reflected, the ideal unit for the jungle. At that very moment, without preparation or forethought, we could set out on the two-thousand-mile journey to Venezuela or on the one thousand miles to the mouth of the Amazon, quite self-sufficient in the wilderness. I should be helpless when cartridges and fish-hooks gave out, but Kaluana, who could make a bow or canoe, whose sense of direction needed no compass, and who knew how to catch tortoises, rats, and snakes, would have been as much at home a year's march away as he was this night by the Kuluene. "Civilizado," he would have said scornfully to any suggestion so pointless, but nevertheless, together we were the lords of the forest. A man alone in the jungle is a man without insurance, open to the whim of accident, but two men striving

towards a common purpose possess the ultimate weapon—
organization and intelligence.

I should have said, of course, not "we two," but "we one
and a half," for I was only one stage from an invalid. Our
mastery was in Kaluana's complicated skills and traditional
knowledge as an Indian, which would take me years to
acquire. Just about as long, I reflected, as it would take to
understand the mysterious and complex man that he was.
To begin with, why had he bothered to teach me? Not once
had I bribed him with a present, and unlike other Indians
he had never asked me for anything that was not essential
to a hunt—matches, fish-hooks, and Terylene thread to
feather his arrows. In fact, he seemed to need nothing now
that he had a gun, machete, and fishing line. Other Indians
would go to Vasconcelos to steal or to the Air Force Post at
Xingu to-work for the bright things that the Caraiba used
as trade goods. But not Kaluana. Once, another Indian had
told me that someone had stolen six knives from his bag and
Kaluana had heard us talking about it.

"It couldn't have been me," he said, "I don't want anything. Or not anything besides a woman's dress." (For the
mistress of his latest affair.) In the Aweti mind, theft was
associated with a specific want and not with a general economic need.

If he wanted nothing, however, why was he taking me?
Altruism is completely foreign to the Indian mind, and by
now I had stopped Kaluana's snatching and using my gun.
Yet every day we would put our game together and crouch
beside it on the ground like two jackals on a kill. Kaluana
would pick out a bird, holding it by two red claws that had
curled into talons at death. "Will you carry this, Adriano?"
If I said, "Yes, I will carry this bird, Kaluana," that meant it
was for the post, though the tail feathers were his traditional

perks. But though the Aweti hut had as many mouths as the post; though I had two hundred cartridges and Kaluana only a treasured three that were charged and recharged with powder and shot; [1] though it was his skill that was the foundation of our success; my burden was always heavier than his.

Why was he generous?

Once Kaluana had been fishing in a little creek, swinging every catch out of the river in a swishing arc, so that the leaping flash of silver whipped round his head and dashed itself to death on the water. His line had slipped and a four-pound piranha with jagged scales had crashed into my nose, cutting open one side of the nostril. It made a gory sight and, on my return, the Indians at the post suggested: "You did not stop running when a tree was before you." But Kaluana was unnecessarily disturbed, almost as if he had attempted to shoot me. He fished for five minutes and then asked if it was still hurting. He hauled out another piranha and then suddenly offered me a tiny mirror. "Would you like to look at your face?" he asked. Finally, he hauled himself up the bank. "Kaluana must see your face now." He had asked me if I would ever go hunting again.

Was that it? Did he need an assistant in the forest?

A few days later he had come to me in great secrecy and had taken me to a log close to the edge of the Vasconcelos clearing. It was, he explained with flattery, to be he and I and the other of the three young Aweti warriors who had a gun, Acouete. I was to pay for the privilege by getting salt, an outboard motor, and gasolene, and we would go for two days up-river till we reached the old site of the Aweti village. That village, I knew, had been abandoned only a few years

---

[1] Most of the Indians who had guns also had brass cartridges that were recharged hundreds of times. Ordinary paper cartridges were reckoned to last three or four firings, Eley-Kynoch eight to twelve.

before when the wild, unpacified Txikao tribe had defeated the Aweti and Orlando had summoned them to live in the clearing by his post. No one, Kaluana had said, was to be told, and I was to bring as many cartridges as possible.

The morning after we set out, when we were eating hard fish that had been roasted the night before, I asked Kaluana if no one ever went back to the village which had been the Aweti home for so long. He had just described it to me. "It is four days by canoe this way on the Kuluene. And three days by canoe that way on the Tuatuari. Then walk. It is a beautiful place and I played there when my mother was alive."

Acouete said that the Aweti seldom went back to the village, but then Kaluana suddenly lifted his face from across the fire where he was eating the flat head of a piranha. Did I know Vatacu, the old Waura, who now lived with the Mehinaku tribe? I did. Did I know that he had gone on a long journey to find salt? I said that I had seen Vatacu's wife and another woman carry the salt wrapped in banana leaves up from the canoe. Did I know then that Vatacu had seen smoke in the Aweti village?

I did not. I asked whose smoke it was, and the answer came slowly and very quietly.

"Txikao."

An uneasy suspicion crept into my mind.

"Kaluana, why did you ask me to bring so many cartridges?"

He crunched deep into the fish that he was eating. "Orlando is savage if we shoot Txikao," he explained. "But if we shoot just over their heads to frighten them a little bit . . ." He paused to let the idea sink in. "After that perhaps we could kill a deer. Orlando likes deer."

The raiding party against the Txikao had come to a sudden end. I insisted that we should return, though Orlando

later suggested that it may have been just a game on the part
of the Aweti. Perhaps it was.

But as we were going back, I asked Kaluana why the
Txikao came over to kill the Aweti and why they had shot
the Mehinaku chief in the back so that everyone could see
the scar when he walked.

"Like you and I," was the reply, "the Txikao like hunting,
travelling, and raiding about the forest."

Once again, I felt that maybe this was a clue to the Indian.
His village was gone, his tribe lived in a Caraiba clearing
and only had one hut. They no longer danced all afternoon
from dark door to dark door, the men no longer painted
themselves and wrestled in the sun. "Why do you dance and
wrestle no more, Acouete?" "They are all dead, Adriano."
"Why do you have no chief any more, Acouete?" "We have
a sort of chief, Kaluana's father. And Kaluana is a little
chief." I think that meant that the "royal" line had died out
and that with such a small group it was hardly worth having
anything more than men of influence.

The tribe seemed doomed and Kaluana might be the last
of the line. "Do you want to get married, Kaluana?" "I want
to get married only a little bit. Not now."

Over the weeks I had begun to feel that in his complete
devotion to the harsh ideal of a warrior, there was a quality
of nobility, some unconscious defiance of fate. Other Indians
met the challenge of civilization by craving its goods and
working for the Caraiba. Not Kaluana. He accepted the
machete and gun which helped his hunting, but his ideal
was unchanged. Most Indians were content to live on fish
which could be caught with line and hook at ease. Kaluana
would hunt all day without a rest or drop of water. Like
a Don Quixote he met the challenge of modernization by
standing upright in the ideals of the past. The motive—if it
existed at all—was unconscious, but I felt that when the

four old men dressed in rushes danced to the beat of chant and shack-shack so that the dead of the tribe who lived under the water would come and pass amongst them, Kaluana wanted the dead to speak like this:

"Do you see the tiger over there. Do you see Kaluana?"

"Yes, I see him. I see the tiger called Kaluana. Who is he?"

"He is a warrior like we were, an Aweti."

And if Kaluana were a Don Quixote, what would he need but a Sancho Panza, though in this case the Don was the tiger and the Sancho the goat. Other Indians could not be bothered to hunt much, but here was a Caraiba who did not talk all the time about how wonderful the Caraiba were and who admired the Aweti skills. He was prepared to act as a pack animal for "cannon" and do as he was told—because this was what the Aweti did in the forest.

I picked up some wood from under my hammock and spread it evenly over the fire so that the blaze would not "become savage" and burn the mutum.

Of course, if my idea about his mental rigidity were right, Kaluana was doomed. Rigidity in the face of this sort of challenge invariably means destruction for a primitive man. But then there were several things to cast doubt upon my interpretation. To begin with, Kaluana was neither a staunch friend not a predictable character.

When we had been coming back from the Txikao raid, the little outboard motor had broken down. After twenty minutes' paddling Kaluana had announced that we would walk. I had refused. Other Indians might steal the motor, and it would be very embarrassing to return to the post without the boat. "Oh, I left it somewhere in the jungle," I would have to say; "We'll fetch it some time later." No! It was out of the question. I paddled on, but Kaluana paddled

Bebcuche winnowing

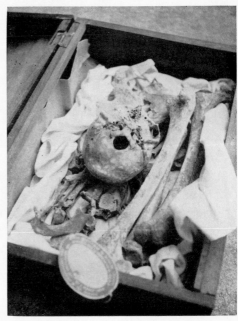

The bones discovered in the "Fawcett" grave at the Kalapalo village

"The Seven Cities": a formation of eroded rock which probably deluded Fawcett into believing that the lost Civilization of Atlantis was concealed in the jungles around Xingu

Kamayura tribesmen beating and spreading the liana poison, Timbo; a bark canoe rests on the barrier to catch fish leaping from the trap

The Kamayura village. The men's shelter and bench are on the left and the dead chief is buried under the logs in the center

The traditional Urua dance of the Kamayura tribe

against me to the shore. I pushed off again. Kaluana pushed back.

For the next three hours, I had to paddle up-stream alone.

"Are you savage?" Kaluana called over my shoulder.

"Yes."

"Then I am savage with you." He had sat whistling in the back.

Three days later, however, he had called and offered to march with me in the night to another village for a feast that would come in the morning. I was flattered, but two hours after we set out, when we had almost reached the village, he slipped back into the forest.

"If anyone says was that Kaluana you were walking with, you say no."

"Why?"

"I don't know." He entered the village another way and avoided me all day. With other Indians I would have hazarded an explanation, but for Kaluana that was impossible. He was completely unpredictable—so bewildering, in fact, that I gave up trying to puzzle him out and spent the rest of the evening wondering how many of the mysteries at Vasconcelos could be put down to the raw material of the Xingu problem, the Indian himself.

. . . .

That night Kaluana came back with four large fish and told me that others had got away with his hooks; we lay in our hammocks dozing and chewing strips of meat from the pile that lay between us.

At midnight it was cold and we both climbed out of our hammocks to crouch beside the fire.

"Kaluana, today I saw a deer."

"Where did it sit?"

"In the roots of the big tree by the lake where you shot two jacubim."

"I have seen a deer there too."

For the next five hours we lay sleeping and listening for sounds in the forest. At morning we would slide into the mist to kill where those clues would lead us.

7

CLAUDIO ARRIVES

ONE DAY BETWEEN hunts with Kaluana, the slow rhythm
of waiting was broken by the arrival of Claudio Villas Boas.
He had spent the incredible period of three years in the jungle cutting a trail from the airstrip of Cachimbo to the airstrip of Cururu, and I watched him step from the aeroplane
with his shirt drooping out of his trousers and with his san-
dals flopping about his feet. He walked at his own pace towards the post, a strange tubby shape with no more baggage
than a flour sack slung over his shoulder. He looked like
Dick Whittington after a rough night. The Indians whooped
to see him.

Some weeks before, Orlando had told me that Claudio
had once walked for twenty-eight days through unexplored
country with no more food or baggage than a .22. But this
was not the man the story had led me to expect. Where
Orlando was a baked Indian brown, Claudio's pale com-

plexion had the green tinge of a forest shadow. Where Orlando had a sharp bold face, he was chubby, wore glasses, and had the mild demeanour of a country grocer.

At lunch that day he sat at the other end of the table.

"Your airstrip is too short, Orlando."

"It is 800 metres."

"That is 200 metres too short."

Orlando demurred.

"It is. I know. Aren't I your brother?"

"Yes," said Orlando.

After lunch, Claudio retired to his hammock and for the next week I hardly saw him leave it. "How does he keep alive without eating?" I ask Juan, and was told that, camel-like, Claudio stored up on food and sleep and then needed no more for long periods. I was intrigued and watched with care. When he did eat, I noticed it was at night, from the left-overs in the pans, so that we seldom saw him. He would scrape away in the dark and munch quietly to himself. During the day I would see his small and bearded form confined to a hammock, listening as Indian men and women came to put their crawling babies on his tummy. They then conversed in the low and endless monotony, which is true communication with a Xinguano mind. Between visits he would read short sections from a pile of books and pamphlets on the ground below him and stare thoughtfully at the roof for an hour or so before his hand reached out and the next passage continued. Once, I looked at the titles. There were several works by Jacques Maritain relating Aquinas to the problems of the modern world, Bertrand Russell's *History of Philosophy,* a polemical pamphlet by Stalin, a heavy book on the significance of Communist development in China, and some reflections by a Brazilian man of letters on events during his lifetime.

When people had told me that, of the brothers, Orlando

was the man of action and Claudio the thinker and philoso-
pher, I had pictured the somewhat tedious backwoods sage
of American literature, brimming with wise saws and quips
to the discomfort of everyone around. But gradually, as the
months at Vasconselos passed, I was to realize that nothing
could have been further from the truth.

When Claudio expressed his views they burst forth in
hour upon hour of rushing, cascading, pouring talk. He
spoke very quickly, digressing through the philosophers. He
used Rome and other historical examples. He argued, thundered, exhorted. "Look at history." "Didn't Aristotle say so?"
"It's obvious, isn't it? Yes." For me it was metaphysics at
race-track speed, in a foreign language, on an empty stomach, under a beating sun. I would gasp and be swept away.
The Indians would stand around curious at an excitement so
out of keeping with the calm tone of forest conversation, and
I would sit amazed at a man who was as much a symbol of
mental passion as Descartes crouched over his famous stove.

But in the early days we barely talked, for in the post we
tended to live isolated lives, each man tied to a hammock and
his own particular duties. A week after Claudio's arrival, Orlando grew tired of waiting for supplies that never came and
flew out to Goiania. I learned from Claudio that the long
delay was the result of a combination of causes—incompe-
tent officials, political opposition to the budget, shortage of
planes during a drought crisis elsewhere in Brazil, and the
difficulty of getting government departments to work together when out of touch in the jungle. The delay was now
in its eighth month but the five Brazilian labourers who
grew the rice at Vasconcelos and lived in little huts to one
side of the clearing had not been paid for two years. Some
bureaucrat had simply forgotten that they existed, and Orlando hoped to return with twenty-four months' worth of
back salaries as well. "I am just going for three days," he

said before the fuselage door slammed; and for the next five weeks messages came back explaining the problems and insisting that the next plane would bring him in person.

With him, Juan flew out to hospital never to return again. He was a very sick man with hernia, malaria, deep eye-aches, and much troubled in the head. He left looking fragile, but with manners still exquisite to the last—of all the people I was to meet at the post, the only aristocrat, incessantly gallant in defence of some hopeless cause. The precise nature of the cause was impossible to define, but no one could live at the post without warming to his vague but noble heroism.

Of the original expedition team that had started waiting in January, I knew that two men had already left. Now that Juan and Orlando had gone as well, none of that party remained. With the labourers and the Indians, Claudio and I settled down to wait.

Some days after Orlando's departure, I was sewing up a shirt on a rest day before hunts, when Claudio came and sat beside me on a log at one end of the clearing. It was early morning and I began to inquire about some of the things that puzzled me in Vasconcelos policy. I asked why the Txikao tribe, only five minutes away by plane, had not been pacified, and Claudio told me that they lived on an arm of the Jatoba River and that to get there it was necessary to descend the Kuluene to Morena before going up the Ronuro River.

"The journey takes a fortnight," Claudio explained. "The first time I went, my two Kamayura warriors and the old chief of the Waura were frightened as we entered Txikao country. They said they had sad memories of their families and returned home. I went on with two Kayabi Indians who took me to the edge of the village. There, Adriano, I saw something very interesting. The haircuts, the ear-rings, the body paint, and the huts of the Txikao are very like the Xinguanos."

The deduction, according to Claudio, was obvious. At some time in the past the Txikao had belonged to the same cultural group.

"I gave my gun to Cerilo, one of the Kayabi Indians, and told him to fire in the air if I was in danger. Then I walked into the village saying all the different Indian words I knew for friend.

"Everyone—men, women, and children—ran for the jungle; arrows came out of the bushes. I moved step by step backwards waiting for the gun to give me a chance to turn and run. Two Txikao jumped out and stood with bows in the clearing. I shouted for Cerilo to fire. Some more men came out with arrows aimed. I took the risk and dived for the trees. As I and the Kayabi ran for the canoe—I could hear shouts and men running behind us—Cerilo asked if he might fire the gun."

A few days later, two Txikao were seen to land higher up on the river bank, where they began cutting what looked like arrow hafts. Instructing Cerilo once again, Claudio made a detour through the trees to come upon the man from behind. Creeping slowly round a bush, he almost crashed straight into one of the Txikao, crouching, and as startled as he was. The man had no bow. Just as Claudio was holding out a knife to serve as that crucial first present that is a link between civilizations, and can change three thousand years of development, Cerilo arrived and made a masterly appraisal of the situation in a flash. The gun roared. Claudio has not seen a Txikao since. "Cerilo can be trying sometimes," he explained.

A short time after this first attempt, both brothers mounted a full-scale expedition. But the village had been moved, and before they could find it, food and gas ran out and the expedition almost starved. Soon afterwards, Claudio said, civilizados had shot Txikao and the Txikao had ambushed a group of civilizados.

Curiously, among the complex reasons for this sudden "civil war" was a flaw in the national constitution. By Federal law no Indian land may be sold without a special act in the Assembly, but by the Constitution, Brazilian land sales are made by the independent State governments which also gain the proceeds. Some of these governments of the interior were beyond all conception freebooting and corrupt[1] so that just before my arrival at Vasconcelos they had opened fire on each other with Sten guns in the Assembly of the State of Alagoas where politics is a battle between the great feudal families. One state governor recently feathered the family nest and carried out four hundred judicial murders before he was unseated. And so no one was particularly surprised when the state of Mato Grosso suddenly acted against Federal Law and sold the right to resell vast blocks of Xingu

[1] Much of this information came from the political correspondent of a Brazilian daily newspaper. In general, Brazilians are much more prepared to discuss the faults of their country than Englishmen. The foreigner only has to abandon his "Holier-than-thou" attitude and to admit that every state has its deficiencies, to be plunged into all the passion and excitement of Brazilian politics. "You are almost a Brazilian," they say, and the argument begins to rage. It seems to me that one of the reasons that graft and influence are perhaps more predominant in Brazil than they are, for instance, in England is the personal nature of everything that happens in that country. Things are only done for the friends of the friends of the boss, and between friends presents naturally pass. But it also seems that the reverse side of this national characteristic is a very real virtue. Brazil contains Negroes, Indians, Japanese, Syrians, and Europeans, and yet it is the only country on earth that has really solved the race problem. The people are immensely friendly, regarding each other as persons and not in the arbitrary sub-divisions of race. As someone put it to me, "In South Africa, and your colonies, the politicians tell the police to shoot the blacks. Their problems get worse. Here the politicians shoot each other. Our problems get better."

to eighteen land speculation companies. The price varied around half a crown an acre, for though no buyer would be able to work the land within a period of fifty to a hundred years, the strips of paper were valuable chips to gamble with on the stock exchange. An Indian Protection Service survey estimated that the cost for the actual settler when he did come would have gone up 3,000 per cent; the *Correio da Manha* published a document in which the Speaker of the State Assembly of Mato Grosso had refused to carry out the duties of his position unless ten of his family were granted a total 200,000 hectares (about 500,000 acres). But the speculation companies were undeterred and sent in surveying parties. (Land roughly mapped has a higher price than land which is undefined.) Since the Air Force and Foundation runways could not be used, the groups had come from Cuiaba and canoed down the headwaters of the Kuluene and Batovi.

One party had machine-gunned a group of Txikao. Another party of twelve had been wiped out by Txikao. Then Orlando had learned of the invasion. Tribes had been warned not to kill, but to give no food. Vasconcelos canoes had searched up and down the rivers, and soon the Indians all over the "kingdom" had become increasingly dangerous. The surveyors began to starve as the Air Force froze every airstrip in the region and confiscated their supply planes. Finally, several of the parties, without food or gas to get back the way they had come, struggled in to surrender, naked and famished, at the Air Force Post of Xingu.

It was, in a small way, a victory for the Villas and the Federal government, but on the other hand almost all Xingu had been sold in the speculation market of São Paulo. The politicians who supported Vasconcelos immediately tabled a bill to create a national park in Xingu the size of Belgium that would provide a living for the Indians in the region.

This would have automatically invalidated land sales covering an area greater than all the property in England. It aroused strong opposition. The Speaker of the Assembly was a Mato Grosso man; the vast land speculation interests lobbied the deputies; and five years later the bill, though undefeated, had still not been passed.

Vasconcelos, which seemed so peaceful to me as I waited for the expedition, was in fact concealing strange and violent forces under its surface. Many Brazilians were working for its destruction; the land under my feet had been sold years before. And though the Indians were fighting on the frontiers against civilizados, they too added to the explosive atmosphere of Xingu. Strong forces within the primitive nature of jungle man were working towards their own death and destruction.

8

DEATH WISH

CLAUDIO OFTEN talked about the Indian problem. We
would sit on logs or home-made benches, and in the time-
less hours of jungle waiting our words seemed more continuous than the days themselves. Conversations broken by
sleep or hunting would pick up without reference to the
delay between. Claudio would be pacing up and down. "The
point that follows from my last deduction," he would begin,
and within a matter of seconds we would be deeply involved
in another of his long philosophical discussions. The sun
would beat outside. Occasionally, Indians would stare gravely
at our talking faces. In their monotonous life, conversation—
even unintelligible conversation—was a matter for respect
and observation.

During one of these discussions a young Trumai tribesman came into the dining-hut, embraced Claudio and sat
down. Indians are like cats. They can sit in silence and still
sit in company with you.

Claudio looked outside at a few Mehinaku warriors making ready for the dance.

"Why aren't you dancing?" he asked.

"I don't understand how to," replied the Trumai.

"Liar. You are clever. You must know how to dance. You have a big head with four tongues inside it—Aweti, Mehinaku, Trumai, and Matipuhy." Claudio paused a second. "Where are the Matipuhy tribe now?"

"They are gone."

"Have they gone to the Kuikuro village?"

"No, only . . . " I didn't catch his name, "is there."

"Where are the rest then?"

"They are over there." He pointed in the direction of the Mehinaku village. "No one lives at the Matipuhy village any more."

"The Matipuhy are dead then?" (Both Claudio and I knew the answers to these questions, but they are the necessary lead-up to a point in Xinguano conversation.)

"Not all are dead. The village of the Kuikuro has one, and the village of the Mehinaku has . . ." He held up two hands and bent down one little finger.

"But you," said Claudio, "son of the Trumai chief, are married to the daughter of the chief of the Matipuhy. Why don't you build a hut where the Matipuhy lived. Then you will start a village and be a great captain."

The Trumai smiled shyly.

"You won't go?"

He smiled again.

"Why won't you go, my son?"

"I don't know." The Trumai stood up and walked gravely away.

"They are killing themselves, my people," said Claudio.

"They seem to want to die."

In all the corporate memory of Xingu there are only two

known cases of suicide. But then suicide is barely necessary
to the Indian. He has the wild animal's ability "just to lie
down and die." Soon after the Spaniards first reached the
new world in the West Indies, tribesmen were captured as
slaves, supplied with good food, given no opportunity of
suicide, and yet died so fast that, home-grown product ex-
hausted, the planters imported Negroes from Africa. The
deaths they believed were analogous to a wild animal's
pining in a cage. Then, various conquistadors and explorers
noticed that when an Indian broke his leg on a hunting trip
he would sling his hammock in fatalism and pass away long
before pain or hunger could have brought about the end.
And recently, on the convoys carrying West African troops
to India during the 1939–45 war, a similar thing began to
happen. A doctor, who is now a Harley Street specialist
in tropical diseases, told me that the Africans under his care
had neither been as primitive as the Indian nor had they
been suffering from any shock of first contact with white
men. Yet when they reached the storms and ice of the Cape
of Good Hope, those with flu would lie down, tell the doctor
they were going to die, and pass away without cause dis-
coverable in post mortem. Hypnotic death was his explanation, and he said that he had been able to reduce the death
rate by seventy-five per cent through visiting the men every
half-hour, talking, and holding their hands. This broke
some form of trance and also gave the men a feeling of care
and homeliness which attacked the root of the death wish.

"The Tsuia tribe have already vanished from Xingu,"
said Claudio. "The Nahukua and Matipuhy are almost gone.
The Aweti have one hut, no dances, no chief. The Trumai
and Yawilapiti are down to twenty. The Kamayura when I
first came had twelve huts. Now they have five."

No doctor lives within two hundred miles of Capitao
Vasconcelos, and so a post mortem to establish death without

THE HEART OF THE FOREST96

understandable cause has never been carried out. But civilizados who have worked at the post during an epidemic have
seen the Indians apathetic, despairing in sickness, making no
effort. They die where a fighting and wilful man would live.

"These people will not help themselves," Claudio said
sadly, and we looked across at the Trumai warrior who was
watching the Mehinaku dance.

A death wish is not easy to explain, even for a psychiatrist
working on a co-operative patient. For inexperienced men
trying to peer across the chasm between the civilizado and
the primitive, the task was impossible. "We haven't the
right words," Claudio said, meaning that the Indian had
never sat down and reasoned about his life, and therefore
had never altered it to logical conformity. Hence, when we
the civilizados put the matter in the conscious and logical
terms of words in sentences, we were trying to explain a
mind by a method that was inconsistent with it. Music,
legend, action, these are the Indian expressions of philosophy.

Still, by that stage of the morning, two jacubim had been
plucked for lunch, fish were ready for dinner, my shirt was
sewn up and the 12-bore oiled. The sun, I noticed, was still
young and its rays were striking a tangent on the bent backs
of the dancers.

Gradually, our talk wandered away and around the subject again.

"The Kamayura," Claudio said, "used to come here to
eat our eggs and chickens, and so Orlando and I gave them
a dozen hens to begin a flock for their village. Then when
they came again we said, 'Why eat our eggs and chickens?
Eat your own.'

" 'We have no more eggs and chickens!' The Kamayura
looked very sad that day.

" 'Don't you like eating them?' we asked.

" 'Yes, we like eating them and now that they are eaten they are gone,' they explained politely.

"So Orlando told them that he had heard a cock when he was last in their village, and they said, 'That is a cock. You don't think we would eat cocks. They sing.'

"It is another way of thinking, Adriano, completely different. What can we do about that?

"Do you realize," Claudio went on, "why we don't grow mandioca here? It is because the Indians eat it. Every year when they dig up their own roots they could easily plant the shoot for the next year, but they don't. Only when their crop is coming to an end, do they plant more and if they don't plant enough, they steal ours. They never think of the future. They are different from us—even about the simplest things."

Claudio went on to say that if no one had ever really understood why primitive people die on contact with civilization, it was because it was so difficult to penetrate the primitive mind. Bullets and disease obviously killed Indians, but it was not so obvious that other facets of our civilization could be equally dangerous. A tin pot was a benefit to civilized man, but it could be destructive in tribal society. Western religion was the greatest gift we could offer, but unless it was given with extreme care it did little more than destroy the tribesman's own understanding of his universe whilst putting nothing understandable in its place. The spirit of Vasconcelos policy was to study the Indian first and only bring to him those parts of civilization that were acceptable. Elsewhere in Brazil, altruistic missions were so obsessed by the divine right and urgency of their own idealism that the Indians were smothered to death by a wave of entirely miscalculated kindness. The problem demanded above everything else one thing from the man who wished to help.

Claudio said it wistfully. "A desire always to understand."

There the discussion ended, but on the next day an aeroplane flew in an American lady on a visit of a few hours. After weeks of jungle life without a plane, we thought she appeared like a miracle in the morning, looking as out of place as a ballerina in a potato field. She was, however, a kind, generous person, probably connected with some relief organization or altruistic society.

"Young man, could you please ask that native to take his trousers off for a snapshot. I want it for our appeal circular. You don't think so? Why that's a real shame."

"Well then, tell me why he wears that red paint. It's to look nice? The same as face powder and lipstick? Is that so?"

"But listen here. I know something about Indians myself. My cousin lived with cannibals in Brazil. You say there aren't real cannibals in Brazil, only the ritual eaters of human flesh? No, I don't know about that. They may be only ritual now that they're civilized, but when my cousin was there they were real genuine cannibals."

It was a curious piece of chance that at this moment a canoe beached and the eldest son of the Mehinaku chief stepped ashore. His flesh was a crawling yellow after three months of incessant concealment from the light of sun. Around his right leg, half-way up the calf, was a deep ditch in the flesh as though burnt with a red-hot poker, and below it his leg was blue and black and purple. Rough lianas, I knew, must have been tightened there like a tourniquet for some weeks, and now that they were off, the initiation ceremonies were probably nearing the poison drinking. Last time, four months before, he had been completely paralyzed, but a swift flight to a hospital outside the jungle had saved him. The doctors had said he must never take poison again.

The boy peered through the logs of the Vasconcelos hut, moving in a circle to get a better view of different parts of the interior. When he saw Claudio, he went round to the door.

Soon afterwards the American lady departed, but on the next plane day another visitor arrived. A little man got off the Dakota and, with a bright and birdlike gait, tripped towards the post. One Indian carried his bag, another his box of oranges.

As he arrived at the entrance, he turned to look at the Indians behind.

"My toilet case. Where is it?" His voice was like a canary's. "Where is eet? The Indians have stolen my toilet case." He leaped nervously up and down and then rushed off to find "who is the chief here," taking nervous swigs from a waterbottle that hung by a key chain from his belt. The Indians looked after him curiously.

Eventually, Claudio asked the Indians if they had seen the toilet case, and one of them said that only two things had come off the plane and both were now at the post.

"Impossible. Impossible. These Indians are thieves. And what shall I do now? I have no soap and won't be able to wash." It was no time to comment on the advanced Vasconcelos views on washing. I led him away to lunch.

The visitor greeted rice and beans with extreme gloom, and two days later I saw him pay an Aweti some hooks for a small fish he had caught. Pioni cooked it and it was served to him during lunch. "This lack of variety in the food is bad for me, so I caught this. But, for you, look what I have brought. An orange to squeeze in your water."

Only the five labourers and I were at lunch that day, and for a group of men that had few pleasures and worked incessantly they were beings of extraordinary dignity. They were also charitable, and each put a little squeeze from the orange into his mug.

On the first night, the little man slung his hammock close

to mine and soon astounded everyone by a cacophony of excited whistles and high-pitched wheezes, which we were forced to conclude were his version of the common snore. I unhitched my hammock and slung it outside between two trees, forty yards away, and woke with dawn to find an Indian seated by my hammock.

"Why does Adriano sleep in the forest now?"

"I like the stars," I said, "and my sleeping bag is very warm."

The Indian smiled and held up his finger. "Listen!" Across the forty yards that separated us from the hut a delightful sound, new to the jungle, possibly to all human experience, tripped and trilled like an asthmatic thrush.

But that afternoon I hitched my hammock inside the hut and out of the sun. Soon after, the visitor's bony finger prodded me in the small of the back.

"Let us talk. Eh? What do you think of the world situation?"

I replied that I couldn't really, because there were no radios or newspapers at the post.

"But do you think it will improve, or get worse?"

I replied that most people seemed to think it would get worse. That was obviously what was expected of me, for the little man launched into his theory. He was a great psychiatrist[1] from Rio, and after years of study he had concluded that all the evil in the world was produced by mentally unbalanced people. I was invited to look at Hitler, to look at Mussolini, to look at Napoleon, to look at Richelieu, to look at Cæsar. If he could train enough psychiatrists to balance all the unbalanced people, he could achieve the paradise.

---

[1] In so far as these conversations relate to a serious problem, it is unfair to present the other side of the case through the medium of the "little man." Unfortunately he was as he is described. That the visitor was a qualified psychiatrist, however, we had on his word alone.

"And do you know what I have come here to do?"

"No?"

"I have come to get evidence to prove my theory."

I was very interested. I said that as he was studying evil in men, he should hear about Claudio's idea that Indians had a selfish understanding of good and bad to themselves, but only a negative concept of bad to other people. There was no positive good like our idea of charity. This meant that an Indian knew he was doing wrong when he left his wife to starve in contravention of tribal duty, but when he saw a stranger dying to whom he had no obligation, he would often pass by without a thought.

The visitor became as a tiger in argument.

"Impossible. Impossible. Impossible." The hammock ropes vibrated with his emphasis. "If there is bad there must be good. If there is white there must be black. It is logical, isn't it? Answer me that."

"But nothing here is logical in the Indian mind as it is with us. His mind is so unlike ours that all the fundamental assumptions that are necessary to logic seem to be different. The only thing people can do is to discover what exists and then try to understand why. There are no 'must be's' or 'should be's.' "

The tiger was in hot pursuit.

"What is black is white, and white means black. Isn't it so? It is so, isn't it? White. Black. Black. White. You have been to a university and you don't understand this?"

I went to ask Claudio to explain. I knew that it was one of his chief laments that occasionally great anthropologists had come to Vasconcelos: "They bring a special folding table and a green canvas stool, and their assistant makes the Indians line up in a queue. 'What is the Kamayura word for mandioca,' they say. 'So and so,' replies the Indian. 'So and so,' writes the anthropologist on a white card with squares on it. 'Who carries the mandioca from the field?' 'Woman,' replies the man. 'Woman,' writes the anthropologist on a blue card with lines. But do most of them ask why the woman carries the mandioca, whether modern influences will change this, and what effect this will have on the Indian's chances of survival? No. They are clever men with good education who could help us, and all they do is to sit on little chairs and write the Kamayura for mandioca."

I thought he would be interested in the little man's more imaginative approach.

9

TAMUAN

AS THE WEEKS go by at Capitao Vasconcelos, the months of the calendar are forgotten and day and night cease to form jointly a date in a year of 365 days. They become separate periods of dark and light that are unrelated in activity or meaning to each other. "When the sun was in the middle of the sky during the last dying moon," the Indians say, to name a moment in the past. It was hard not to sink into their way of thinking.

For longer periods than the number of moons that can be counted on the fingers of a single hand, the tribes of Xingu measure the passage of time by the development of a human life. "From the day when a woman has child in her stomach to the day it first cries," is a common phrase; "when my son was this high, till he was that high," is another. And so it was not unnatural that, like the Indians, I came to measure my period of waiting by the growing up of a little boy.

Tamuan was a Trumai Indian, and though nobody could

say for certain, he was probably eleven years old. His father was dead and his mother's family no longer cared. Orlando had taken him into his hut, and the other Indians who lived there had been asked to look after him. They were young men of the Txukahamae and Kayabi tribes whom Orlando had brought to Vasconcelos from the lands in the north.

"Tamuan is my brother," Pioni the Kayabi told me when I first came to Vasconcelos, and I noticed that the two Txukahamae Indians sang songs for him and that afterwards he would tell them that they were the best singers in Xingu. Pioni taught him to kick a soccer ball, and when I went underwater fishing, Tamuan would sit in a canoe above, giggling helplessly. I explained to him that some fish were quick as deer and fled as soon as I entered the water, but that others were as lazy as sloths and sank into caves to wait till I glided by. "Adriano is pouncing on the lazy fish," Tamuan would shout, "but he is lazier than the fish himself." He found this immensely funny and would roll about on the bottom of the canoe. He seemed the sort of cheerful little orphan boy you could find in a displaced persons' camp anywhere in the world.

Then, sometime in July, a major in charge of parachutists loaded his platoon into a plane and set out to drop them in the most difficult area of Brazil; the plane flew into the jungle and thirty men came floating out of the Vasconcelos sky, hanging on to large pieces of cloth. The Indians were phlegmatically unmoved. As children accept a clown, Indians accept the civilizado. Anything can be expected of the Caraiba. They collected arrows, bows, and headdresses; bargaining for trousers and boots began.

It was only Tamuan's young mind that was deeply moved. Here in the sky was adventure and beauty that Indians had never known. He borrowed my handkerchief; Claudio found some thread. We all carved little bits of wood into sergeants and corporals and even made aeroplanes that would discard parachutes when thrown into the air.

"Parachute! Parachute!" Tamuan would shout as he stood on the bluff, watching a piece of cloth drifting towards the water. "The major," he giggled, "is going to fall in the water. Hooray, the Caraiba is going to get wet." At other times he would stand on the ten-foot platform where Orlando had put a Dakota gasolene tank for water storage, and leap off holding the post's only tablecloth.

"Tamuan will grow up a Brazilian," one of the soldiers remarked before he left. It was an unusual and significant comment.

At Capitao Vasconcelos the civilizado has to get used to the idea that the tribes around him are dying. Emotion or frenzied action can only bring harm and he soon becomes insulated to the tragedy with an artificial but necessarily matter-of-fact attitude. But this little boy who had played in our hut all summer? It seemed hard that his future should be so bleak. I began to wonder if the soldier could be right and whether for Tamuan, at least, the problem might not exist if the Indian could become a Brazilian.

A few days later, I was sitting on a home-made bench at the western end of the hut. The sun was falling on one of the three magazines that I had brought from Rio, and a cold wind was coming across the marsh and whistling over the floor. Tamuan came and sat beside me. It was common knowledge that when reading I was fair game. The dogs had the pigs to tease, the Indians had me.

"That's water," he said, obstructing the page and pointing to an advertisement. (Indians can always recognize people and objects, but can seldom differentiate between landscape, water, and sky.)

"And that's a big canoe," I observed, pointing at the liner that an insurance company deemed a mark of symbolic security.

Tamuan looked at the picture carefully. "It's a big canoe," he said. "It's bigger than that house."

"It's got houses in it to sleep in and shops and restaurants and churches."

"It could be Aragarcas," said Tamuan, who had flown to the settlement with Orlando.

"It could be."

"Is it going fishing?" Tamuan asked.

I looked for another picture and fortunately found one of Christmas in England. Everything was covered with snow.

"It's going to my home," I explained. "It is so cold there that all the rain and water become solid." Tamuan giggled at my conceit. Not even a boasting Indian would claim such magic for his country. "If the river were in England," I said, "you could walk across it."

"Like you, when you swim with the flippers?"

"No. Walk properly like this." I strode across the room.

But before Tamuan had time to express his doubt, the post's tame jacu fowl started to speed round and round the room with little legs flailing in the sand, trailing its wings to either side to trim its balance while taking corners. It went on for four to five minutes.

"Why is the jacu doing that?" I asked.

Tamuan giggled. "It does that because Indians are coming."

I thought on this for some time. "Where are they coming from?"

"I don't know. Maybe down the river. Only the jacu knows."

"How does it know?"

"It hears them. In my village when the jacu runs we go

outside to wait for the Indians at the edge of the village."

An hour later they arrived, almost the whole of the Trumai tribe, and I was forced to eat the words of doubt I had expressed at Tamuan's statement. For a week the Trumai were to camp in the forest by Vasconcelos, visible evidence of the ignorance of the English civilizado.

"Let's go and pass the time with the Trumai." Rauni the Txukahamae would say, and taking Tamuan we would go and sit on the ground beside their fire to listen to their tribal songs. They were calm songs—as Benedictine plain chant, but more monotonous.

But every time we returned to the post, Tamuan came back with us. "Don't you like the Trumai?" I asked. "I like them only a little bit," was the reply. "I like most Rauni, and Pioni and Claudio, who is my father."

Two weeks later I sensed some sort of a stir amongst the Indians and noticed little groups of Aweti talking to the Trumai and some Kamayura who had just come in that morning. Pioni told me that "they are going to make earrings for Tamuan and two other Trumai boys." As I knew that the Trumai had no initiation ceremony (this had not yet been absorbed into their culture), I guessed that the Kamayura "Druid" would do it for them.

"Why are you going to be initiated?" I asked Tamuan.

"The Trumai say it is beautiful," he replied. "I am going to have toucan ear-rings."

That night the dancing began.

At the sound of a deep chant, I went over to the hospital hut. It was almost black inside and before my eyes had adjusted themselves to the darkness, Kaluana's father seized my arm. I found myself dancing with the rest. Two paces forward, two paces back. Two paces forward, two paces back. Dual lines of men facing each other going backwards and forwards, backwards and forwards to a monotonous, dirge-like chant. Each of the three boys was held firmly between two men.

The women stood arms linked in a semi-circle to one side, moving their right foot backwards and forwards and occasionally coming in with a low agony of a sound, so deep that it was almost unbelievable. It was the most primitive thing I had seen or heard in Xingu, and I imagined that the marrow in my bones was shaking. It was as if the very nature of Indian womankind was groaning in sexual passion at the arrival of a new warrior who would keep alive the mystery of the womb and the tribe within it. Deeper, deeper their voices went. The chant went dull in my ears, smoke choked my throat, dust turned to mist in my eyes. Earlier I had noticed that the ground shook with stamping and that the leaping flames cast strange lights for a moment on a thatch wall, for another moment on a net hammock. But very soon I noticed nothing at all. There was just the chant and the deep craving of the women.

Not until one of the Indians who lived in the post touched my shoulder did I realize that I had been dancing for two hours. I had eaten their food and drink, but Xinguanos—so far as I know—do not have alcohol or drugs. I had seen no special creeper thrown on to the fire, and yet I had been completely lost for all that time in the rhythmic hypnotism of sound, movement, and light.

That night I slept, but the Indians danced till morning, occasionally stopping to massage the initiates' ears. Then when the sun stood at the finger tips of a man holding out his arm straight from the shoulder, white cotton sashes were tied around the boys' waists and they danced in line to Orlando's hut. There the sashes were taken off and the boys, squatting on mandioca mats, had a lock of their hair cut with scissors. Water was poured down their backs from a tin bowl.

Away they danced again, each boy with a man's arms on his shoulder. Another chant, and the boys were sitting between the knees of "godfathers." More chanting and bamboo sticks were thrust between their teeth. Black paint lay in stripes across their face and arms.

Then, at the hiss of the red-wreathed Kamayura "Druid," a horde swooped on the boys, a swarm of hands plunged and writhed, dust seethed, and the sun beat down on the hard yellowness of the earth. Tamuan had vanished under a score of limbs. I heard no sound. But when the commotion ceased I saw the three little boys, each with a bamboo pin thrust through his lobes, biting against pain on to the stick in his mouth, no blood flowing from his ears because of the massage during the night.

Tamuan had gone. He was now Aruyawe, the name of his grandfather whose soul had come to live in the body of the child.

That night I talked to Claudio about the encouraging way Trumai boys had sat in peace between Aweti legs under a Kamayura Druid, and the discouraging way Caraiba scissors and bowls had entered an Indian ceremony. My real interest, however, was to see what had happened to the little boy who had lived in Orlando's hut. He slept there no more.

For three days there was no sign of him, and then I went over to the place where the Trumai tribe had made a cavern of branches and blankets in the jungle. There, in two hammocks and around a little fire, Tamuan who was now Aruyawe, and another, who was now Kaluene, sat constantly sheltered from the sun. Theoretically, they should have been in a hut like other Indian boys who keep away from the light of day for the period of a year, sitting between the thatch wall and a blanket, fattening on rich foods; at the end of my brief stay at Vasconcelos I could barely recognize children whom I had known at the beginning. The deep brown of an

Indian skin would go the sickly yellow of a consumptive Japanese, and at the end of the year they would emerge to the surprise of the tribe. "Who is this beautiful person so fat and with such clear skin?" the Indians would ask in astonishment.

But that morning it was not Aruyawe who held my attention but two strange chunks of wood he had in his hand. I asked him what they were.

"A drink," was his reply. He rinsed out a calabash and washed his hands. Then scraping a dip in the ground so that the calabash would not tip, poured water into it. He beat the wood with a strong stake until it went pulpy and stringy, and afterwards flicked water on the pulp. The wood hissed and when he rinsed it in the bowl, the liquid foamed like a Tide advertisement.

"What's it called?"

"Cimbo."

"Do you mean Timbo that is used for the fish poisoning?"

"No. A little Timbo. Cimbo."

"What do you want to drink it for?"

"To make me fat and tough."

"Do you drink it every day?"

"No, only now, but when I go to the Trumai I drink others."

"When does it all finish?"

"When I am a man three moons from now. I take out the wood," he pointed at the bamboo pins in his ears, "and put toucan." We then arranged that I, my "cannon," and the Trumai should go hunting for toucan some time in the future.

A few minutes later I saw Aruyawe pick up the calabash and drink half of it. I took a little—cautiously—and found that it had an insipid and soapy taste. Meanwhile, he had taken a white feather, plucked most of it so there was only a tip at the end, and finally tickled the back of his throat. Two pints of cimbo poured out as if from a tap.

"I would have much sickness," he explained, "if it stayed inside." (Recently another boy had been completely paralyzed.)

I saw nothing more of Aruyawe for some weeks. His parachute no longer floated around the post; someone had taken his ladder from the jumping platform; no one asked the two Txukahamae to sing and then told them that they were the best singers in Xingu. But one night there was a hiss from the trees and he was there. Could I get him some rice from the post's kitchen; he was not allowed to go there himself.

"Why can't you come to the post any more?"

"I don't know."

"Where have you been all this time?"

He told me that he had been fish poisoning by the Kuluene River. As he spoke he stood there solid and taller and without giggling.

"What happened to your parachute, Aruyawe?"

"I gave it away—to a child."

He then asked me if I would fulfil my promise and go toucan hunting with him. Tomorrow? Yes! When the chicken first sings.

The result was that at dawn we were deep in the woods not far from the Kuluene when a pack of monkeys went swinging by. Aruyawe slid after them with a borrowed .22 —I had never thought of him with a gun before—and I went elsewhere after other game. Five shots rang out, but when I followed the direction of their sound, carrying the cock mutum I had killed, I found Aruyawe sitting dejectedly on a log. He had put five bullets through the monkey in a high tree but each time had failed to strike a vital organ. The monkey might not fall for a day.

By afternoon, his despondency had increased. We had

seen nothing all day and then when Aruyawe had traced the
call of a jacubim till we stood directly beneath, I had pulled
the trigger and missed. The gun had been my 12-bore; and
the range, twenty yards. Scorn filled Aruyawe to the tips of
his ears.

On our walk back, as we forced our way through the heat
of the marsh that burned and licked at us like a forest fire,
Aruyawe walked behind me. I heard his stomach rumble.

"I am hungry," he said.

"That's good," my reply was wary. "You will enjoy your
fish all the more."

"I don't like fish any more. My woman who cooks for me
is sulking." He paused and then muttered almost into the
back of my neck. "You didn't kill the jacu for me."

"You didn't hit the monkey."

"I killed the monkey," was the reply, "but it ran away."

"Then I killed the jacu, and it ran away too."

We returned to Capitao Vasconcelos in silence, and next
morning Aruyawe left for the Trumai village. I never again
saw the little boy who was "going to grow into a Brazilian."

A period at Vasconcelos had ended.

10

THE END OF AUGUST

A DAKOTA LANDED on the airstrip at the end of August, and as the crew had a few days to spare, they asked if they could spend the weekend at Vasconcelos. Hammocks were shaken out, bags and cases were carried off the plane, and the hut, —usually so quiet—began to fill with bright colours and awaken to the vivacity of new voices. They had a radio, and we heard fresh music for the first time in months. They had brought a cook and special food, sweets and lemonade, vermouth and chocolate. One of them possessed a guitar, and another seemed to be a professional crooner for, sobbing deeply in his stomach, he pushed his face close to yours and smiled for the cameras that didn't exist. There was fishing and swimming in the Tuatuari; there was football on the baked, yellow earth. Conversation scintillated; laughter roared. Who would have known that Air Force officers could imitate an Indian dance? Who could have guessed that they could shoot with bows and arrows? A fiesta was proclaimed. Dancing had come to Vasconcelos.

The first to leave was the post's tame blue macaw; sitting grumbling on top of a tree like a bishop disturbed in a London club, he was shot by one of the visitors. "Look what I have just hunted. An arara." The Indians rolled up their hammocks and went to sleep elsewhere; Claudio retreated to his hospital hut and, in the middle of the second day, I half filled a jerry can with gasolene and called the two Aweti hunters, Acouete and Kaluana. As we were pushing the boat out, Pioni the Kayabi boy, came up. Things were going round in his head. He wanted to come too.

That night our camp was on the left bank of the Kuluene River where the Trumai warriors have made an open cavity in the trees to serve as a fishing site. They had placed two branches as springs to hold a canoe firmly into the bank, and Kaluana was so delighted with the ingenuity of this device that he stood for ten minutes in the mud, pounding great waves of water to test its efficiency. Fish were caught at dusk and slow-roasted over the fire. Then, in the moon's soothing light, we paddled over the water to look for turtles' eggs. The sandbanks were thick and firm under our feet and covered with thin tracery where turtles had climbed out of the water and stumped across the ground to dig. We found the holes they made, each an Aladdin's cave with a dozen pearly eggs that would rumble and germinate in the sun till one day little turtles would emerge and scamper towards the water.

Pioni and Acouete began to rock about, practising Caraiba gymnastics, helpless with laughter, rolling in the magnificent sand; and I thought about those great porcine beasts, the tapirs. They seem the most unimaginative of all animals, and yet they are often attracted by the water and the moonlight to risk death from a hunter by playing and gambolling by the river's edge. Soft winds blew magic tales across all the sandbanks of the Kuluene, bringing talk of emptiness and

Kamayura warriors decorating themselves for wrestling

A Kamayura dressed up for the Dance of the Dead

Ceremonial wrestling

An Aweti warrior

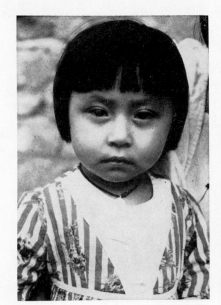

A mission child of the dying Bororo tribe

Two Kamayura boys pounding mandioca

The Dance of the Dead at Capitao Vasconcelos

A Trumai boy sitting between the legs of a "godfather" during initiation. The Kamayura "druid" stands behind, holding a bow and wreathed in flowers

the unknown, of violent and wonderful things that are unheard of in the cities to the east. But, like all beauty in the
wilds, the night was very hard and cold. We returned to our
hole in the trees to lean over the warmth that was fire.

I put a few grains of mandioca "flour" on the blade of my
knife and burned them in the flame—they taste different
that way. The three Indians murmured from their hammocks.

Pioni would say a word in Portuguese, a language common to all three, and then tell them the Kayabi for it. The
others listened and then told the Aweti. As a topic, it could
hardly fail, moving graciously till the name of a bird was
spoken and Pioni wandered away in legend so abstruse that
it was impossible to follow.

The bird had had, however, something to do with God.

"Do you know anything about the Kayabi god, Pioni?"

"I remember a little, Adriano. My grandfather told me
when I was very small, and now only my uncle knows.
[Both Pioni's parents had been murdered.] He lives a long
way away in the Kayabi Cuiaba. But I remember something.
There was a God and he makes all these things in the forest,
and then he is man and other men killed him."

Pioni's section of the Kayabi may have had contact with
the missionaries before they fled into this part of the forest to
start their war with the civilizados.

"Why did they kill him, Pioni?"

"I don't know and I was very small when my grandfather
told me. Then later there was this tree, a very big tree that
many men could not put their arms around and these men
begin to work at it with axes. And when there were many
little woods on the ground," he picked up a twig from under
his hammock and I deduced he meant the chips made by
an axe, "this God came and said to the men that this tree
held up the sky. I don't know if this is so. This is what my

grandfather said. Then the God said if they cut the tree down the heavens would fall and kill them and him too. So the men had fear and picked up all the little woods and put them back in the tree. Then when they passed water . . ."

"Do you mean rain?"

"I don't know. This is what my grandfather told me when I was very little. Then when they had passed one water, the tree made good again, but my grandfather told me that now it is not very strong and creaks. Maybe," he ended, "maybe, it will fall."

Pioni lapsed into speculative thought. I lay with my head in a position where I could see one star between the leaves. Perhaps we would hunt tomorrow, or perhaps fish and turtles' eggs would be enough. Perhaps we would go back the day after, or maybe not for a long time. The months lay contented before us. The expedition's delay had lost its importance. My first troubled weeks at Vasconcelos seemed not months, but civilizations away.

During the night Pioni—who, though seventeen, is unusually nervous for a forest dweller—thought a puma was looking at him from a branch above his head. He whispered to Acouete to pass the .24 bore and fired a cartridge into the beast. Only leaves and twigs came down. "That Pioni," Kaluana muttered from his hammock, "that Pioni is a child."

PART · II

The Centro Expedition

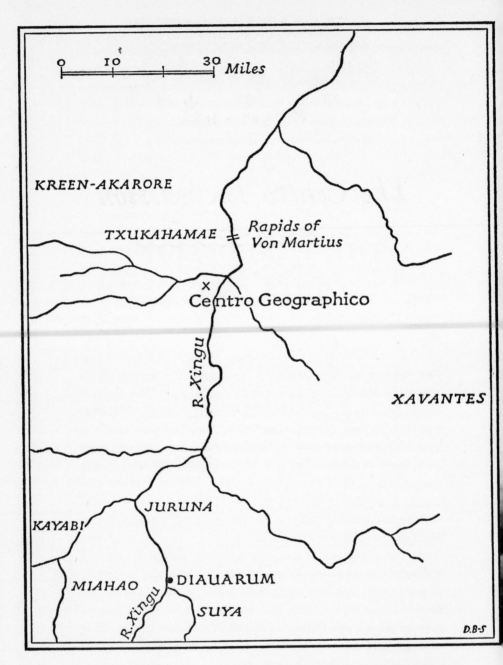

Scale: 0 — 10 — 30 Miles

KREEN-AKARORE

TXUKAHAMAE ⚏ Rapids of Von Martius

× Centro Geographico

R. Xingu

XAVANTES

JURUNA

KAYABI

MIAHAO ● DIAUARUM

R. Xingu

SUYA

D.B-S

TRIBES IN THE AREA OF THE CENTRO EXPEDITION

11

THE EXPEDITION
SETS OUT

FOR WEEKS AFTER Orlando's departure, the sound of an aeroplane would draw a crowd to the airstrip. The Indians would be carrying babies and hoping for presents. "Orlando has brought knives and pans," they shrieked into the sky. The labourers would be in too great a hurry to put down their hoes. "Orlando has our salaries," they shouted at the trees. Claudio and I would follow slowly behind to show that we, at least, had not dropped everything at the first sound and leaped for the runway. "The expedition," we said to one another, "will leave tomorrow."

As the plane taxied to a halt, it was always Rauni the Txukahamae who stepped to the door. "I have sad memories of my mother and brother and the wife I want to marry," he once told me sorrowfully, and I knew that he could not return to his village through the country of the Juruna tribe without Orlando's protection. Every week, Rauni's great paws felt at the door, waiting for the aircrew to release the catch inside, and then his heavy face peered in with the expression of a bear looking into the delights of a dark and hollow tree trunk. His face was the barometer of our spirits. For four weeks it dropped like a lead weight, and on the fifth he walked up to the pilot, sombre with anger. "Why you not bring Orlando?" he demanded. The pilot, confronted suddenly by a strange being with a distorted, wood-plated lip rattling up and down, made a joking reply. Rauni grunted and swung back his rifle. For a second the Indian loomed above the pilot, his gun swinging down to club the civilizado on the neck.

Then Claudio jumped across and grabbed the butt. He was just in time.

But in the sixth week, when all hope had been adandoned, a strange man appeared in the Dakota doorway. His hair was cut, he had a new shirt and jeans, his feet were in shoes, but difficult as he was to recognize, there could be no doubt about his identity. The Brazilian Santa Claus was here. Orlando was back. The whoops and cries spread about the airfield.

Ten minutes later, I passed Rauni staggering towards the store hut with a crate clutched possessively to his chest. "Bowls," he said, indicating his exploratory knife-cut in the sacking. "For my tribe," he added firmly and scuttled possessively on.

Huge 44-gallon gasolene drums thumped and clanged as they rolled down the pathway; Pioni carried several cheap rifles and was wearing a new .22 single-shot pistol like a Texas sheriff. Another Indian staggered under a box of provisions; a Kamayura pulled a sack that was leaking beans; Kaluana had acquired—with accustomed skill—a bundle of clothes that looked heavy but was, in fact, very light. All the supplies for an expedition and all the presents for a great distribution to the people of Xingu were in procession from the aeroplane to the store.

"In three days," Orlando said, "the first boat must leave." And down by the water the old labourer, José, was soon to be seen scraping and caulking the canoes, stuffing in waste and then nailing on a strip of tin from an old margarine can. "Will the boats leak during the journey, José?" "No, Adriano, it was very good margarine."

Our fuel was inadequate to last out the journey, and higher up by the dump the high-octane gasolene was measured out in a one-litre tin of peanut oil by the new riverman just arrived from the region of the Araguaia. He was called José the younger. In the hut and on the table, maps were spread out and heavily marked in pencil.

On the next day a plane flew in with extra men to join the party, and Franklin Gomez, the geologist, brought with him aerial photographs of the Xingu River, recently taken by his firm PROSPEC. These were examined knowingly through magnifying glasses, and everyone discussed them with everyone else.

Gradually the expedition began to acquire some sort of form and shape and the following list was made of its personnel and equipment.

Boats
30-ft. canoe.
2½ h.p. outboard.
1½ h.p. "Seagull" outboard.
Two 20-ft. civilizado boats of shallow draught.
Three 4½ h.p. Penta outboard motors.

Men
Orlando   Official Indian Protection Service Rep.
Claudio   Official Central Brazilian Foundation Rep.

Franklin	Geologist of PROSPEC commissioned by the Government.
Sergio	Old expeditionary friend of Orlando.
Dilton	ditto.
Clementi	Experienced woodsman from Claudio's Cururu trail.
Raimundo	ditto.
José	Riverman.
Jorge	Mechanic.
Pioni	Kayabi.
Cerilo	ditto.
Batacu	Kamayura.
Rauni	Txukahamae.
Bebcuche	ditto.
Adriano	Ingles.

To be added

At the Juruna village   one canoe and two warriors
                                    to pilot the rapids.
At the Txukahamae Village two or three warriors.

Stores

6 live pigs—presents for the Txukahamae and Juruna tribes.

Great boxes of knives, axes, bullets, pans, fishing lines, hooks, etc.—presents.

1 box containing some tinned food.

Sacks of rice and beans.

Salt, sugar, oil.

Other sundries, including a radio.

Preparations were well in hand on the day before departure when a pilot landed with news that Leonardo Villas Boas, the third of the brothers, had been shot the afternoon before on the River of Deaths. It was the first tragedy of the expedition. Claudio flew out to see what could be done, but

Orlando continued to supervise the loading of the long canoe that was to take the gasolene to a supply dump three days down river. The boat would then have to return for more equipment. Three of the expedition were to act as crew on the journey there and back. Dilton de Motta, a member of Orlando's previous Txikao expedition, was in charge and would remain with me to watch the stores at the place of the Black Pumas till Orlando and the main party arrived.

On the following afternoon, Claudio flew in with the good news that Leonardo only had a bullet through his hand. It seemed that a frontiersman had come into a store on the River of Deaths to get drunk on cachaca, a local sugar-cane alcohol with which it is possible to purchase complete oblivion for the price of threepence. After twopence worth, cachacados usually rise up and look for their enemies, and at this stage in the incident a suitable enemy had, by misfortune, appeared in the doorway. The drunk had spattered him with bullets. The enemy had been untouched, but a small girl standing a few yards away was killed and her mother grievously wounded. Then, realizing what he had done, the drunk had moved forward to fight his way out. Leonardo had jumped and in the struggle had been shot in the hand. The drunk had escaped to the jungle.

Killings are sadly frequent in the interior of Brazil, and of the five labourers at Vasconcelos, one had killed a man and another had fled to the post to avoid being shot. And so the discussion did not last long. After a few minutes everyone decided that the expedition could afford to wait no more.

At 2:30 on September 3, our overloaded canoe was pushed out from the Vasconcelos landing-place.

"It floats," said José, the riverman, with relief. "It floats," we all repeated in varying tones of confidence. There were six inches between gunwale and water. The five of us crawled in and we wobbled away downstream, staring peacefully at the

golds and greens and all the shimmering colours of the Tuatuari. Every now and again, the canoe lurched into a sandbank and we heaved and hauled at its long cigar shape till it
slid over into the deep water beyond.

Where the Kuluene joins the Batovi and Ronuro rivers we
found a great expanse of water that wandered mysteriously
amongst lagoons and sandbanks in a maze of romance and
sudden views. The place was Morena, where Mavutsinim
created Indian man and where the first sound of rapids was to
be heard ominously roaring away to the north. It reminded us
that from the direction we had come most of the tribes were
pacified but that ahead only three groups were Orlando's
friends; the rest killed strangers on sight.

At the entrance to Morena we found a long peninsula, like
the jutting snout of a crocodile, and there, on the first night of
the Centro expedition, we slung our hammocks between the
trees. The dark came down. Cerilo, a Kayabi warrior, squatted
at the tip of the shore.

"Savage Indians," he whispered gloomily. This attracted
several of us and we watched beside him for a flash of light
that appeared ghostlike every now and again across the water.
It was concealed by trees and very faint.

"A Suya war party!" Cerilo was mournful by nature. "They
will creep up on us during the night." His heavy face grinned
at the bitter joy of his own impending massacre.

We watched a period longer.

"That's a torch." This came from Dilton de Motta. "A fire
is a redder light and it doesn't move sideways along a bank. It
only moves up and down with the wind. Because they have
never met civilizados, the Suya can't have torches. Cerilo,
you're an old fool. The people over there must belong to
Takuman's Kamayura tribe. They come here to fish."

Cerilo humphed and muttered something about Kamayura
being just as bad as Suya, since they had killed many in his vil-

lage when he was a boy. "I won't sleep tonight," he informed us sulkily; "I know that. I won't sleep." And whilst we snored, this Kayabi Indian put wood on the fire so that the flames made light in the clearing but emphasized the mystery in the dark, forest alcoves around. His tribe lived in the lands ahead and possessed a century's record of war with the civilizados and a reputation for being hard and ruthless warriors; he and three others were the only survivors of an entire section wiped out by civil war. But, despite this, he passed close to my hammock before dawn. "Adriano," he said, "I haven't slept." He scratched his bottom and seemed mournfully cheered by the thought.

Our canoe slipped away a short time afterwards, and Cerilo steered as we shot the rapids that proved to be no more than water that was leaping and turbulent and banging at the floor of the mist. We were lucky that morning, for the fog lifted in time for us to look back at the junction where the three tributaries formed the Xingu River. From our particular point on the globe, everything that man could see or imagine within the distance of his walking legs or his paddling arms was subject to the mystery of this prince—the great river. Its valley was larger than England, and all the hills and land within it had been moulded by the flowing of its waters. Every day, in my hunting, I would walk without fear of being lost, because every dry watercourse leads to a rivulet that flows into a stream that travels to a tributary that must eventually seek the lord of all things, Xingu. I would hunt close to its great banks because animals avoid the barren land to the interior and live on the fruits and leaves of riverine jungle, whilst I would find Indian villages near the river's "high forest" where the soil was rich for mandioca, peanuts, pineapple, and other crops. This great land we did not call the territory of the Xingu River, but just Xingu, and on the journey we described its landmarks in such terms as, "The camp by the third bend after the junction with the bottle-shaped lake." In this way, even our conversation paid tribute to the overwhelming power and mastery of the river.

And so the days passed as we travelled in a hollowed tree-trunk canoe, pushed by an outboard motor, and helped by the current's quest for the Atlantic. All the lagoons, islands, and openings on either side made it difficult to realize that we were not floating on a landlocked lake. Everywhere the river seemed to end in a confining wall of dark and mysterious vegetation. Each half-hour or so we would come to a twist in the bank or opening behind an island to see the river running on once more into what looked like yet another dead end in the forest. And our course was even more tortuous than the stream itself. For with the dry season the water had dropped, leaving huge mile-long sandbanks that forced the river into channels of swift-flowing current. Upstream from these sandbanks, Cerilo steered as far away as he could; like icebergs, they sometimes reached out a quarter-mile underwater. Downstream, however, it was possible to pass two feet away, as the cliff of sand would drop sheer to the bottom, cut harsh by the sweep of the river. From side to side we went, backwards and forwards, sometimes heading south when I knew that our course must be north, often steering for what looked like a blind alley in preference to a great sheet of water leading into the distance. The river was bewildering to the beginner.

And so I sat barefoot, jeans in long shreds from knee to ankle, and my hat very crushed from acting as a pillow at night. The others had suggested that there were enough hazards in the river without my steering as well. When we stopped, game seemed to stand at the end of our guns, fish lived wherever we threw our hooks, and tortoise eggs were so plentiful that half an hour was enough to collect the five hundred that glistened in the bows. Cerilo slept curled up on a gasolene drum, brooding about the Suya who were watching us from either bank. José muttered to himself by the motor, and Dilton stared through his binoculars, looking for animals on the shore. Once we saw fourteen very tall jaribou storks sitting grouped in pairs. "This sort of stork is always married," José explained, "and the women storks never let the men storks go away by themselves." Large capivaras—rodents that look like water-rats and are bigger than pigs—crouched on the banks and watched us go by. And occasionally a turtle or giant otter would pop its head out of the water to blink cynically at our strange and hopeful passage. Mark Twain, I thought, had been wise when he had given Huckleberry Finn freedom from his civilizing widow by letting him float on a raft dirty, without preparation or ambition, unloved, undiscussed, disorganized, in blissful abandonment to the slow movement of the Mississippi's current.

At eleven o'clock on the third day out, we saw some tall palm trees in a grove close to the river. It was Diauarum which is the Indian name for "The Place of the Black Pumas."

12

THE PLACE
OF THE BLACK PUMAS

TWO MEN STOOD by the shore as we drifted into the landing. Orlando had told us that half a dozen years before he had cleared an airstrip here and that occasionally people were flown in to keep the runway cut and level. Behind their figures and up a little hill, surrounded by palms and cackling hens, we could see a few log-and-thatch huts.

The men were strangely silent.

"Good day!" Dilton explained that we were to dump gasolene for Orlando's next expedition.

"Good day!" There was neither friendship nor enthusiasm in the reply. The men helped us to land the drums, gave food to Raimundo, Cerilo, and José, and then pushed the canoe out for its return run to Vasconcelos.

Dilton and I walked up the bluff to the kitchen.

For men marooned six months or more, our hosts had an unusual apathy towards the outside world. Daniel, one of the three, had not left the kitchen to watch our boat come in—it was perhaps the first for a year. When Dilton gave out the news, their interest was not very marked. Another big expedition was leaving under Orlando's leadership. Yes? Brazil had won the world soccer championships. Oh? France was on the verge of revolution. Is France near Europe?

Within half an hour of our arrival, conversation dropped back into what we came to know as the normal tempo of Diauarum life.

Leopoldo was the oldest and, as the unofficial chief of the establishment, sat on a black wood bench that had been much worn since it was cut from the forest five years before. The puppy's plate—a tortoise shell—was by his feet. "So, Ferocious"—Leopoldo had a soft voice—"so, you're frightened of a little piglet. An Indian dog like you that has to grow up to fight pumas." He tweaked the animal's tail with his big toe that stuck out from his foot like a gnarled, but flexible, potato.

"It was the little brown pig that chased him," said Daniel from beside his clay-brick stove. "He chased the big cock too. He's a little pig, but very valiant."

"And only a month old," Leopoldo went on. "The litter was after we killed the uncle pig. He was fat, so fat that he snored at night and kept us awake. Three bins of cooking-grease we had from him that will last us a hundred days. I washed an empty bin out yesterday, so that means it is just more than a month. Only a month old," Leopoldo prodded Ferocious, "and an Indian dog like you is frightened of him."

And so the talk went on, slow and very peaceful, in a hut that reminded me of sixteenth-century engravings of a serf's hovel. On the two sun-side walls, the chinks between the logs had been roughly filled with mud to keep out the heat during the day. Inside, there were little hand-carved stools, home-made racks for plates, knives, and mugs, and also a table. A clay pitcher held water; fish and meat dried in the sun on a rack out of doors; and a parrot sat above our heads. The bird started to shriek and Leopoldo chatted back, provoking it into an outburst of spluttering Indian words. "You don't speak Portuguese yet, eh? You unlearned Indian parrot."

Later we were shown an airstrip four hundred yards long and learned that the duty of the men was to defend this from the enveloping jungle. A plane, in theory, came every one or two months. "It is always late and sometimes it forgets," he said, as though it were a half-trained and unpredictable animal. "When it remembers, it never remembers everything, and so for weeks we are without food—especially in the rains." To guard against this, the men cultivated a clearing in the forest which lightened the aeroplane's supply load and guaranteed that if it crashed they would not starve. "Look at my little orange tree." Leopoldo fingered its leaves between his thick thumb and first finger and told us that leaf-cutting ants had destroyed his previous young trees. "No poison had been able to stop them. But then I saw these little ants on a stick fighting the big ants. They were valiant and strong like the little pig. So I took some and saw that they did not eat the leaves. Every day, I took some little ants in my hands to the tree and they always went away. But one time they did not run away, and so now they live here and fight the big ants. The tree is growing and there will be fruit next year."

Leopoldo's work had probably been in vain; with the cut across the North Mato Grosso just completed, the closing of the airstrip was under consideration. But at that time no decision had been reached, and the slow placid life between the runway, the plantation, and the huts, measured only by eating, sleeping, and the regular spasms of work, continued day after day within the confining wall of the jungle. Since Orlando eventually arrived, not on the expected fourth afternoon after the canoe had set out but a fortnight later, we had plenty of time to see, yet again, how well this type of man, called the caboclo, is suited to his jungle life.

. . . .

The name caboclo, strictly speaking, means a half-caste of white and Negro blood, but in the Mato Grosso the word seems to be loosely applied to more or less anyone of the labouring frontiersmen class. They are the men who work for the Central Brazilian Foundation; Orlando had three caboclos on his expedition, and caboclos as his labourers at Vasconcelos. The rubber tappers lower down the Xingu, the frontiersmen on the River of Deaths, and most of the invading surveyor parties were of this class. With the Indians, they are the human ingredients of the war in Xingu.

Most of caboclos in North Mato Grosso come from the cattle plains of the North-East of Brazil. During the many drought and famine periods in this region, cattle can be seen dying all over the grey dusty bush and men sit limp in hovel doorways, while sad mothers watch children pull at breasts that are yellow. It is a country of despair where a hundred eyes follow a stranger in a village street, not the eyes of inquisitive men, but just watchers watching. Life in a face is a rare thing, and expression is seldom to be seen outside the little hovels where a roulette wheel, marked for the illiterate with pictures of cattle and animals, spins throughout the day. People seem transfixed by a wheel that, like the seasons, quite arbitrarily decides man's fortune and fate. And just as the losers are forced penniless from the gambling room, so, with every famine, more and more men are driven to risk everything in the forests of the Mato Grosso.

A typical story is that of Raimundo, one of the boatcrew that brought us to Diauarum.

"I left in 1943 when I was young to get rich in the Mato

Grosso. For us in Maranhao, Adriano, the Mato Grosso is the land of riches, and at home there are too many people and too few jobs. All the jobs go to men with influence. So when I heard of this diamond mine in Goiaz, I went." Raimundo had a small eager face creased with lines of disease and hardship.

He told me that he had worked there for some while and then passed on to a crystal mine where the earnings were better. "At first we had a good patron. He gave tools, clothes, and food. Always rice and beans, mandioca flour and dried meat. And coffee and sugar were plentiful. He was not one of those who, when you are not finding much, looks at you with a hard face and grumbles about the food. He took fifty per cent and we took fifty per cent, and often we sold our fifty per cent to him. But then he sold the mine to another. A strange man, Adriano, almost mad. He wanted to make more money by exchanging the crystal for oil and he exchanged our crystal too." Raimundo then explained passionately and in detail that the patron had lost on the deal and had expected the miners to suffer with him.

"The man was raving, Adriano. Waving his revolver."

"Did he shoot?"

"Shoot? He shot at me." Raimundo bounced up and down on his seat.

"Did you shoot back?"

"Shoot? I ran, Adriano. I ran and left the mine and I ran and went to Aragarcas. It was a hard journey on foot and by horse and cart. After a year I went to Xavantina, where I worked for the Central Brazilian Foundation for four years. Then for the Air Force at Jacareacanga for three years, and I went on leave to Santarem where I spent my money. Girls, drink, dice—Santarem is made for men." Raimundo spat. "I came with two years' salary and I left with none. There I also lost several good offers for jobs, one for 2,800 cruzeiros [$22 a month] with Sabba."

"Working in the forest?"

"Yes, working in the forest. And when I returned to Jaca-reacanga my post was gone and the Air Force sent me to Xingu. There I talked to Claudio, who offered me 2,400 cru-zeiros [$19 a month] to work on his trail, and there I worked for two years. And now I am here, Adriano. On Orlando's expedition."

Living in the same hut as the three men at Diauarum, it was hard not to feel that the caboclo was the salt of the earth and the human foundation that would one day make Brazil a great nation. Born in poverty, inured to hardship, paid $11–22 a month, the caboclo is prepared to work in the jungle without hope or comfort. He is humble, kind, immensely courageous, and though bustling foreign contractors have railed at what they regard as his laziness and slowness, it is only because they do not appreciate the tempo at which he works. For a salary, a caboclo sells his entire life, endurance and courage, becomes a retainer, will fight for his master, is prepared to struggle for years working and living off what his gun and hoe can win for the stomach. But, because he is the raw material for the struggle in Xingu, it is also necessary to understand another more explosive side of his character. Perhaps violence is engrained within him; he has centuries of repression within his blood and grows up under the in-cessant heat of the North-East's desert sun. Whatever it is, the caboclo, so placid in mood, has deep within him an urge every now and again to gamble all life on one heroic feat, to venture on some fabulous journey of hardship in the forest, or to risk everything sailing the great seas of the South At-lantic on rude balsa-wood rafts—jangadas. As the traveller passes through the North-Eastern villages of Brazil, he sees these men sitting idle in the dust before their hut doors, limbs bent about as if composed for a cubist painting, expressing black temper in the very tension of their stillness.

All the time we were at Diauarum it was impossible not

to sense the eruptive power beneath the surface. (Daniel later threatened to kill Leopoldo with a .44 carbine.) Only one thing was needed to create the classical situation of trouble between pioneer and jungle man—a tribe of neighbouring Indians.

. . . .

The Place of the Black Pumas had, for a long time in the past, been the home of the Suya tribe. It was an ideal site for a village, standing on a little bluff above the water, and possessing the most fertile soil and the biggest concentration of a wild nut called pequi on the whole upper Xingu. Naturally, the Suya had been reluctant to leave.

But roughly a generation before, the Txukahamae tribe had set out on one of their nomadic wanderings. They travelled up the Rio Liberdade, cut across the watershed between, and burst out of the forest to massacre whatever Suya happened to be in the village. This onslaught was followed by a further attack that captured most of the Suya women, and then by a later raid from the Trumai Indians. This tribe complicated the situation by fleeing afterwards to the protection of another Indian group, the Waura, whose monopoly of the pot trade gave them enormous diplomatic influence. For decades, the Suya had relied on the Waura for pots and now, with this trade menaced by the new change in alliance, the Suya position was desperate. The shortage of women promised an end to the supply of young warriors for the future, and the absence of pots would restrict most of their traditional methods of cooking and storing food.

A solution—almost Machiavellian in character—was found. Someone in the Suya council must have pointed out that the Waura women were also manufacturers of the tribal pot. The result was that suddenly, one day, the Suya attacked without warning, captured several droves of these pot-making females, and abandoned their own village for a hidden retreat on the upper reaches of the Suya-Missu River. All hopes of trading with the Waura were thereby destroyed. "But why," the Suya must have said, "do we need a trade in pots, when we have stolen the factory itself?" With women and earthenware the tribe was content, and since then its members have rarely been seen.

Once, when the Villas had been building Diauarum, Claudio had sighted two Suya in a canoe and had paddled after them through the flooded jungle, only to lose them in the vegetation. Recently he had flown over their village and had counted four huts with a probable total of one hundred men, women, and children. Otherwise the tribe was unknown.

. . . .

Five or six days after my arrival at Diauarum, I decided to abandon the areas where the caboclos shot their game and paddle out into the Xingu to canoe up towards the Suya-Missu River. It was a Juruna-type canoe, hollowed from a tree trunk, and better than a Kamayura "woodskin" for the heavy chop that was blowing across the water. After some time, I turned up a little creek below the main mouth of the tributary. Eventually, this came to a shallow end. I landed, tied a liana to the prow, and left the canoe lazily swinging with the wind. In that tree-lined alleyway of water, it seemed a symbol of perfect peace, and yet in Xingu where man is rare, it was as loud a proclamation of purposeful human presence as a nineteen-gun salute. A canoe at that place meant man hunting and therefore man armed.

I wound my way quietly through the trees, listening for

game, and saw for the first time in Xingu a sort of bear about the size and shape of a dachshund with a long pointed nose and very sharp teeth. It was a coati. It watched me pass with extreme suspicion.

A little while later, following the exact line of my creek, I managed to cross a deep mere on a fallen tree trunk. Under my weight the wood squeezed bubbles out of the mud with a strong, gaseous smell that clung to me till I came out on to the bank of a narrow fiord-like lake. At the far end, a clump of duck took off heavily with a laborious beating run along the water, while nearby a big stork flapped from the shore to sit in a tall tree. Fish, two feet long, leaped in that peaceful lagoon; it was as murderous an arena for survival as any part of Amazonia.

It was about half-way along the north-western bank of this water that I found the fire, a group of black embers at the end of a log and a bare patch of ash-coloured soil.

I began to prod about the bushes. Three or four minutes later, I turned up a broken Waura pot. Indians of the Vasconcelos group, I knew, never travelled to this part of the forest and yet there was the pot, indubitably Waura in its size, texture, and characteristic outward turn of the lip. I noticed, however, that it did not have the fine red polish and black painted design of the typical Waura product. Could this, I wondered, be a separate evolution on the part of the daughters of the Waura women stolen so long before? Was this, in fact, Suya earthenware? I sat down and pieced the bits together till I had what was almost the whole of one pot and a few fragments from another. A large party indeed! Indian men, travelling alone, seldom carry pottery, and when they take their women with them, several are prepared to cook in the same pan. Two pots would normally only be necessary for four or five families and a probable total of twenty people. What, I wondered, had a score of Suya been doing

fifty miles from their village and so close to the post of Diauarum?

Sitting in that pleasant stretch of forest, I remembered Orlando telling me that he had once found a pile of pequi nuts
cracked and littered around a tree close to Diauarum. The
men helping to build the airstrip had disowned them and,
after pacification, the Juruna tribe admitted to creeping into
the groves. They told how one warrior had been cracking nuts
when he heard Orlando coming. Without any other retreat,
he had climbed into the tree and bent the palm leaves
around him so that Orlando stood unknowing beneath. If,
I thought, the Juruna had been tempted by pequi with more
than a dozen civilizados at Diauarum, might not the Suya be
prepared to take similar risks with only the three caboclos?
This place was an ideal camp site with water and fish from
the lake, cover from the high trees, and a position fairly close
to the pequi groves. The fire did not seem to have been rained
on. That would time the visit since the last rainfall at the
beginning of the pequi season. My theory seemed possible. I
set out looking for clues.

The lake, I discovered, eventually came to an end, but the
high bluff on the north-west side continued till it led me to another lake and then to another and another in what seemed
to be a chain leading on from the creek where I had landed
the canoe. Along the rib which formed the north-western
bank of this broken waterway, I began to suspect a trail.

When first I had come to South America, I had seen
straight paths running through the forest swept clean of every
leaf and had assumed that these were Indian-made. In fact,
they had been highways cleared by the leaf-cutting ants. By
contrast, this trail looked barely used and was hard to distinguish from the rest of the forest. It was a track in so far as a
series of faint dents and impressions followed each other
along the ground, and the dead leaves—from being previ-

ously trodden on—did not crackle under my feet. Perhaps it was just an animal trail; all forest close to water is criss-crossed with them. But, gradually, as the path continued, never going down to the shore and following a definite line along the bank of the lakes, I realized that its origin must be human. Then I saw that saplings were broken every now and again at the height of a man's waist; this is a common and almost unconscious Indian habit for marking a route. Obstacles that an animal could pass under were side-tracked; tree trunks that a man could step over bore no mark where an animal would have put its feet. It must be an Indian trail.

Then, after the seventh lake, the forest broke out on to the Suya-Missu River and the puzzle was solved. During the rainy season when the tributary burst its banks, the line of lakes obviously served as an overflow into the Xingu via my little creek. And now, in the dry season when the water was low, the bank made a clear and easy way through what was otherwise "dirty" forest.

"I think the Suya paddle down the tributary," I told Dilton de Motta that night. "They must leave the canoes to avoid coming into the open on the Xingu River. Then they go to the pequi along these lakes."

Next day, Dilton came with me to investigate.

It was an eerie morning with a faint wind stirring the trees so that branches creaked and it was difficult to guess the origin of the noise. A few clouds were in the sky and the sun would suddenly disappear, plunging the forest into an ominous darkness. Two fowl clattered away, shrieking their fear across the lake.

We padded along, examining the trail. Every now and again I would point out the various signs that I had seen the day before, and Dilton would whisper his observations upon them. He was by no means convinced that the track was Indian, but true to the atmosphere of the day and the ominous

woods, he spoke in low, sibilant tones. I looked amongst the
trees and wondered about an encounter with the Suya.

At the second lake, I peered across a long stretch of fetid
scum to the farthest bank. Was that the shape of a man, that
silhouette hidden by the jungle's curtain on the other shore?
I stood still and watched. If it was a man, what would we do?
Creep round the lake? The Suya would hear us. They would
either melt away into the trees or lay an ambush. Perhaps it
would be better to . . . At that moment the sun came out
and my man was revealed. It was a rotten tree trunk leaning
vertically on a log.

We proceeded on our way.

As our investigations took us deeper into the forest, I became increasingly conscious of Dilton following behind.
When a hunter is walking alone he automatically allows for
the sound of his own passage as he analyses the noises about
him, but the creak and crackle of a friend is like a scrambler
on a radar screen. The noise was unnerving. I felt as if I was
walking blindfolded through the forest.

Suddenly, when we were half-way along the trail, Dilton
hissed at me. I heard a faint rustling in the distance; we both
crouched tense behind bushes. It was a light, regular sound
that came closer and closer, a hurried, trotting, I-am-going-
somewhere noise which made me breathless with the excitement of listening. I knelt and found a gap in the foliage. I
heard a click as Dilton did something to his rifle. Then between the leaves of my bush and through the other scrub and
stumps that separated us, I saw a file of shadows flit by, curiously light and athletic in the swift movement of their passage.

"Forest pig," Dilton laughed. It was noon. They were going to water.

Though I went back to the trail many times more, I never
encountered one of the Suya tribe.

13

THE SERINGUEIRO
KILLINGS

A FEW DAYS LATER, Orlando's flotilla appeared in the distance of the Xingu's great bend above Diauarum. For a long time it was just visible, moving slowly across the water, and then the big canoe came in, steered by José. Some time afterwards, there was a volley of revolver fire from the other boats. They had run out of gas and drifted in—somewhat shamefaced—thirty minutes later.

As the canoes were unloaded, Orlando told us that seringueiros (men who tap wild rubber in the forest), were setting out flour poisoned with arsenic on the lower Xingu, where they hoped it would be found by raiding Indians. They had already succeeded in killing forty of the Kuben Kran Kegn tribe.

In our turn, we told how a group of Kayabi Indians had passed through Diauarum some days before. They had said that they were having no trouble with the seringueiros on the

western border of the forest, but that the Juruna tribe had recently killed two. This was obviously a serious matter and
more important than any chance of trouble with the Suya. My
trail and pots would have to wait for a later expedition, and
after breakfast next morning we set out to deal with the Juruna problem. We moved quickly down the river, using aerial
photographs—taken recently by our geologist's firm—to de-
tect and avoid the sandbanks under water.

By late in the afternoon, a great pillar of smoke was black-
ening the eastern part of the sky.

"Indians?" I asked, apprehensively.

"Juruna. The village is after two bends in the river."

Orlando then told us that the only other Indians in the
neighbourhood were the Miahao, two days up a river called
the Manitsaua-Missu. The name of this river meant the
water of the tribe Manitsaua, who had since disappeared, and
it was possible that they were the same people as the Miahao. (This word was simply the Indian for "the tribe whose
name we do not even know.") None of the Miahao had
ever been seen by civilizados or spoken to by Indians in contact with civilizados, but Sergio, one of the party in my boat,
had seen their smoke on a previous exploration.

He had set out with one Juruna and a friend of Orlando's
called Murillo.

"Then I saw a puma, a beautiful black one, Adriano, just
on the bank, looking at me. A puma is the only thing I had
never shot. I fire with my rifle. Bang. The puma falls into the
water and begins to swim." Sergio told the story sitting on the
gunwale opposite and jerking the handle of the motor so that
the boat zigzagged across the river. He had a leathery face
and a very black beard.

"I have never killed a puma before, and I want the skin.
So I swing the handle of my little two and a half [outboard]
and I aim the canoe for its head. The Indian stabs with his

arrow and just then, by the luck of disaster, we strike the puma. The Indian falls, the canoe tips over, and Murillo and I, and our gasolene, and our food, and our guns—everything —we all go to the bottom of the river. Poosha." Sergio grinned.

He told me that in the confusion that followed, he struggled to get back to the motor and found that the puma's instinctive reaction had been similar to his own. As Sergio was scrabbling with the stern of the boat, the wounded puma crawled on to the canoe's upturned bow. "Poosha. I look at the cat and he looks at me and I think I mustn't let the motor go to the bottom of the river. But Murillo gets to the bank and holds his revolver up like this." Both Sergio's hands held the butt of an imaginary revolver before his eyes. Our boat zigzagged even more. "Murillo shoots six bullets and one of them passes through the neck of the puma. Bang. He dies."

Since then, no one else had had sight of the Miahao. Half an hour later our flotilla swung round the last bend of the river and the Juruna village was before us, clearly visible in the distance from its criss-cross of white streaks where feet had worn the vegetation to the pale sand beneath.

Preparations were made to herald Orlando's coming to this part of his domain, and I watched the process with interest. The method involved several rockets, as thick as a thumb, eight inches in length, and held in the right hand out away from the body.

"Let's see what they do. Wait till my binoculars are ready."

A match was struck. Whish. Whish. Boom. Boom. Boom. Rockets whizzed and soared all over the river, exploding like thunder and shattering the stillness of the forest air.

"They're running," Orlando said from his binoculars. The Juruna—not unnaturally—were diving for the forest.

But when our boats were close enough to be seen from the

shore, the Indians came to the edge of the bluff and answered the greeting with a welcoming shot of their own. They stood, thirty to forty men, women, and children, grouped around Bimbina, the chief, who was a great broad man wearing a garment like a furniture remover's leather apron. He held a wooden club that seemed to be a mark of his rank.

We all shook hands, all of us with all of the Juruna. And though no word was said, it was obvious that both Orlando and Bimbina were watching to see how the situation would develop. A few days before, two civilizados had been murdered, and though justice has no place in an Indian mind, revenge for murder is an essential part of tribal conduct. We might be expected to retaliate.

Up the bluff we walked and into a hut that was almost entirely filled by a great obstacle in the centre, with only just enough room for a man to pass. When the bamboo covers were drawn off, it proved to be two large canoes entirely filled with fermented Indian beer. I drank, pleased to have something to cover my nervousness. It was the usual tribal beverage prepared by the chewing and spitting of women, but it was of a slightly sour variation, something like the taste of rough cider. It was a pleasant drink, if you forgot its origin and manufacture.

As we were sipping from our calabashes, the Juruna stood about dark and silent. I noticed, for the first time, that an Indian face when not deliberately expressing friendship does not have the softness of a European's in repose. The spirit behind it is different, not necessarily ill-meaning, but hard, born to violence, and prepared to kill without a thought. I asked for another calabash of "casiri" and drank it smiling inanely, patting my stomach with affable gusto.

Soon after, Orlando broke the tension by leaving the hut for a conference with the chief and elders. "They were fright-

THE HEART OF THE FOREST 144

ened that I would be angry," he explained when he came back. "So I said that I was their friend and not the friend of the seringueiro. Then they told me."

Two civilizados, bearded and carrying .44 Winchesters, had some days before debouched in a canoe from the Manitsaua-Missu into the Xingu. In itself this was interesting enough, for the Manitsaua-Missu had previously been used only by the Villas Boas. It was the ideal back door into Xingu, and obviously as news of the pacification work had spread, the old deterrent—fear—had lost its power.

As the two civilizados had appeared at the mouth of the Manitsaua-Missu, they had been seen and had faced the danger by landing at the Juruna village, saying that they had come from the rubber areas across the watershed to the west and were hoping to descend the Xingu and Amazon to a town a long distance away. (Presumably Belem.) They had been allowed to continue their journey.

A day and a half later, the two men had returned to say that, as the voyage was long, the Juruna must provide them with food. The women—all the men were away hunting—said there was no food in the village. The seringueiros had threatened that unless everything was ready next morning, several people would be shot. Then they had slept on one of the island sandbanks where the Juruna normally retreat when attacked by the Txukahamae tribe.

"During the night," Orlando said, "the Juruna men came back. If seringueiros threaten to kill Indians, Indians kill seringueiros. They went in canoes and—" He made two peculiarly expressive Brazilian gestures that flicked the thumb and fingers down on to the palm of the hand with a sharp cracking noise. "War-clubs. They buried both, but Bimbina says one was dug up and eaten by a puma."

"The seringueiros were sons of bitches, and Bimbina said he was frightened that I would be angry and kept the rifles to show me. I told them not to be frightened. Orlando isn't angry. He is their father."

The rights and wrongs—if it can be put in such a way—were hard to judge. The Juruna could have twisted the truth slightly to suit their cause; at any rate, two men of our race had died tragically in the forest, as we ourselves might do one day in the future. It was hard not to mourn their fate. But then the seringueiros were almost certainly fugitives from justice to have tried the dangerous Xingu escape route instead of leaving on the normal plane or boat service on the Tapajoz river system. Such a desperate last resort probably meant a murder to their credit in the unruly frontier world to the west.

On the other side, Indians cannot appreciate that killing is a crime. They know that the family of the dead will mourn and seek revenge, but they see this as an automatic reflex of self-defence and not as a desire for justice. To a Juruna, war with the seringueiros is so much part of his battle for survival that causes and motives of a particular killing are usually swamped in the fears and hatreds of an inherited feud.

A few hours later I talked to Siriri, one of the men who did the actual clubbing. Though he knew little of his tribe's history, he had this to say:

"First we lived lower down the Xingu and worked for the seringueiros, but they killed many with rifles. So we came up here past the great rapids and lived till the seringueiros say they are friends and gave us rifles. So we went down the river again and worked for the seringueiros till they killed more Juruna. Then we killed many seringueiros and came back here and killed Trumai and Kamayura Indians. Then the Txukahamae tribe came and killed almost all of us so that we are only twelve now." (He meant twelve warriors, as women and children are not numbered in the count of a tribe.)

From what I could gather, through Siriri's matter-of-fact

description, the Juruna at that time were too weak to have any aggressive intentions. They would kill only in self-defence. But just as the Indian finds it difficult to distinguish between civilizados, so seringueiros must be put out to differentiate between the various warlike and non-warlike tribes. Only two days before, I had been talking to Bebcuche, one of the two Txukahamae warriors on our expedition.

"Do you eat piranha in your tribe, Bebcuche?"

"Yes, we eat."

"But how do you catch them? You can't shoot piranha with a bow."

"No," said Bebcuche. "We kill with hook and line."

"But before Orlando, you had no hook and line. They don't grow in the forest like arrows and the poison for fishing."

"In the forest," Bebcuche insisted. "Txukahamae find hooks and line. Seringueiros have them," he explained. "Over there where the sun goes to sleep, we kill all seringueiros in hut. Then we take clothes and rifle and knife."

"You kill everyone?"

"We slaughter everyone. Man and woman too."

"Why don't you keep the women?"

"Txukahamae only keep children. Much time before we have three girls from over there," he pointed to the east. "They all finished now, but axe and gun and line for fish still good."

Killing civilizados had become an essential part of the economics of Txukahamae nomadic life. Birds were shot for meat and feathers, seringueiros for fishing line.

. . . .

Three days after our arrival at the Juruna village, the fast aluminum boat was sent back to Diauarum, the crew being Jorge, Sergio, and myself.

Orlando's scissors are used during initiation

A boy drinking the initiation poison, Cimbo, which frequently causes total paralysis

He tickles his throat and two pints of liquid pour out

Dilton de Motta with a pot discovered in the jungle belonging to the unpacified Suya tribe

Preparing the canoes and boats for the Centro Expedition watched by a special planeload of visitors

The Jurinia paddled quietly into the night and clubbed the two seringueiros to death. They showed us how it was done a few weeks later

We delivered our consignment of medicines and, after sleeping the night, we waited on the off-chance of meeting the Central Brazilian Foundation plane that should have made rendezvous with us four days before. Then we set off back to the Juruna again.

Lianas and hanging bushes formed a filigree of vegetation on either side of the water's curving shore, and at first one felt like a stranger in Soho. Outside on the river, everything was open and bright as in the neon-lit streets of Piccadilly, but just a few steps across a dark threshold and you would be in a gloomy land as mysterious and savage as any part of the London underworld. But as we gradually sank into the tedious rhythm of travelling, all interest in scenery disappeared. The sun stood brazen in the sky and thundered off the river to pound at our faces. The jungle shrank till it was a mere smudge on the borders of consciousness.

About two hours out, we ran into shallow water by a sand-bank to fill the tank with gas, and there Sergio—a happy-go-lucky humorist—yanked the starter cord so that the boat jerked forward with a burst of motor. Sergio shot head over heels into the water; Jorge and I landed in the bottom. The propeller picked up speed and the boat galloped off on its own.

A few seconds later, I got to the motor. Unused to a Penta, I could not find the fuel control lever.

"Where's the lever?" I shouted.

Jorge must have been deafened by the engine, for he smiled politely at the unheard witticism of this laconic Englishman who did nothing whilst an uncontrolled boat careered wildly across an Amazonian river.

I shouted again.

Jorge entered into the spirit of the joke and laughed uneasily.

I shouted.

Tears of mirth trickled down Jorge's anxious face.

At that moment we almost struck a sandbank, and I leaped at the steering handle, heeling the boat over like a motor-bike on a corner. We both landed in the bottom. "This Englishman," I heard Jorge mutter, "he is crazy like a frog."

When eventually we steamed back to Sergio, he was standing dripping, arms limp in amazement. Volleys of sound whistled at us across the water, describing the motor in virile poetry such as has not been heard in England since the time of the Elizabethans.

An hour later, Jorge was asleep, Sergio was steering, and I was looking down the shore for game. Suddenly, I saw two canoes and nearly a dozen paddlers lying close to the bank, with overhanging branches acting as a partial concealment.

We heeled over in a great surge of spray and swooped down to investigate.

Most of the people were obviously of the Kayabi tribe, but there was a strange Indian who proved to be a Bakairi. There was also a civilizado, a great powerful brute with a bearded and aggressive face, but eyes that were by contrast kind and sensible.

"Going far?" Sergio asked.

"Oh, just up the river to get a plane at Xingu." Casual! Considering that the journey he described meant one and a half weeks' paddling and that he must have spent roughly six weeks canoeing through hostile country to where we found him, it was casual indeed.

"Where have you come from?"

"Down the Manitsaua-Missu. From the Sao Manoel River. It has taken a long time."

"Did you see Orlando at the Juruna?"

"No, we passed in the night." Hmmm! So, the Kayabi must have warned him about the Juruna. I wondered if the strip of paper I had found on a hunt up the Manitsaua-Missu two days before had belonged to this man and not, as at first I believed, to the two murdered seringueiros. Perhaps he had been hiding close by.

"Are you a seringueiro?" Sergio continued the questions.

"Yes. I have been working over there for six months, but now I am finished. I am going home. Rondonopolis near Cuiaba."

Sergio decided to let them go, and we motored off to get Orlando's orders. Now that they had been caught, it was useless to hide, and the outboard could easily catch them again.

"The son-of-a-bitch," Orlando stormed up and down, his beard waving with anger. "If he takes the Kayabi to Xingu without me, the Kamayura tribe will kill them. The Kayabi must come back."

A boat was detailed off with Sergio and Clementi and also Pioni who could talk to his Kayabi fellow tribesmen. "If the seringueiro has promised them presents for the journey, he must give them immediately. He can go on. But not with the Kayabi." Sergio and Pioni took rifles and Clementi his revolver. As a foreigner, I gathered, I would not be welcome. "Ever since Fawcett," Orlando had said previously, "the government is fed up with foreigners getting themselves killed in our forest."

When the party returned that night, it seemed that the situation was as bad as it could be. The seringueiro and his Bakairi friend had gone on to Diauarum without trouble, stripped of practically everything they had—guns, knives, clothes—in payment to the Kayabi for their services. The seringueiro would be safe at Diauarum, but he had left his mark. One of the Kayabi was down with flu.

"This is the worst thing that could have happened," Claudio gloomed.

"It's just a bad bout of colds, isn't it?"

"I have had fifteen years' experience and I know that

nothing delays an expedition as much as flu. People can't work. Indians die. And we have to stay in villages to fight the epidemic."

The problem was that the Kayabi would try to get back to their village, and with no medicine there the tribe would die like flies. There was a discussion and eventually it was agreed that Claudio should stay behind when the expedition set out next day for the Centro. He would nurse the Kayabi at a camp near the Manitsaua-Missu River and try to keep them away from both the Juruna and their own village.

Later that evening when everyone else had retired to their hammocks, I helped Clementi roast the piranha to be eaten next day. They gleamed above the fire and the two of us sat and watched, occasionally turning the fish. Clementi talked about the seringueiros.

"These camaradas have a hard life, Adriano. They are poor. No clothes, no knife, no food, and they are told that if they work for a rubber patron they can have these things in advance for the work they will do. They have no family, no house. They go." Clementi waved dramatically.

"But then when they get there"—Clementi added suspense by stirring the fire—"ah-ha, then they find everything has to be bought at the patron's store and that there everything is dearer than on the Araguaia River. To live in the forest and to get rubber a man needs clothes, pans, a knife, a gun, mandioca flour, cachaca. On the Araguaia this cost ten contos but at the patron's store, ah-ha, it is forty contos.

"So this camarada goes away into the forest and works rubber. So! He works for six months and comes back with his rubber in a canoe. It is not enough to pay forty contos. He goes again. But to go again, he needs mandioca flour and new pans and knives. Thirty to forty contos. He can work ten years and never pay. He works hard and doesn't eat well, because if he buys much food he will never pay his debt. And he can't go away without paying because the patron owns all the boats and planes. Sometimes the patron sends men to beat him to work harder, and sometimes he kills one and runs. So! Like this one today."

Clementi was of the same class as the seringueiro, and his home was between the Rio das Mortes and the Araguaia where many of them come from. With but one twist in circumstance he could have been the seringueiro in the canoe that day.

14

CUTTING THE TRAIL

ORLANDO ROSE EARLY next morning and bustled up and down between the hammocks. "Arise, bottom bruisers of Brazil, the expedition has almost gone." Soon after, the mist cleared and our boats set off downstream.

Claudio stayed behind in the Juruna village. Feeling strangely sad, we watched his dumpy figure till it faded out of sight.

Two and a half days later, with the sun shining overhead and water chuckling beneath our bows, the expedition passed a small island on the Xingu River. Our convoy had moved from one page of aerial photography to another, and we knew that a line drawn due east from the Centro Geographico would cut the river in the middle of this photograph.

The boats were moored a kilometre downstream, and our work began.

Camps on Orlando's expedition were usually no larger than twenty square yards; a few minutes' machete work were enough to clear brush and saplings from between the trees. Hammock supports were chosen with an eye to the track of bees, ants, and termites, and the strength of the trees themselves. Otherwise, the central placing of a portable iron grid on which meat and fish could be roasted was all that was done. Camp took thirty minutes to set up and twenty minutes to strike.

At this place, however, Orlando decided to make a permanent base. "We are to be stationary for almost a month. We will build a tourist hotel." Orlando chose a site where the bank rose six feet above the river and then smoothed out on to level ground, and we set to work with axes and machetes cutting the saplings till a clearing was opened in the forest. Far above our heads, the trees made a roof like the dome of a small cathedral. Piumes—small flies that bite throughout the hours of daylight—swarmed about us, but we were particularly plagued by a small sweat bee called the tiuba. Thirty seconds without movement would collect one hundred crawling all over the body, five minutes a thousand—if any man could stand still that long whilst insects wandered inside mouth, ears, and nose. Great bonfires were made to help keep the bees away.

Then next day we built our hotel! Its supports were tree trunks, its rafters saplings bound by lianas, and on the frame we placed a thick thatch of overlapping banana leaves. Nearby, a similar lean-to was set up for the kitchen, and afterwards we took all the stores into the huts and placed them on a framework of logs above the rainwater level. Finally, a great tree was chopped so that it fell far out into the river to make a washing and swimming platform above the sting rays in the mud. Camp had materialized; our real work could begin.

The geologist, Franklin Gomez, had explained on his arrival at Capitao Vasconcelos that the geographical centre of a country is discovered by the same method as the gravitational centre of any solid body.

"Cut Brazil out from the rest of the world and stick it on a pin at its geographical centre," he said. "If we do the job properly, Brazil should pivot like a top." The calculations had been made by an organization in Rio; it was Franklin's duty to find this mathematical spot in the great unexplored regions of the forest.

At first his problem had been Xingu's existing maps based on the explorer von den Steinen's sketchy nineteenth-century information. Rivers were marked where there were none, and all the tributaries were shown as dotted lines, which meant that any guess as to their course was as good as the cartographer's. One of PROSPEC's aeroplanes had therefore been sent over to take aerial photographs and afterwards had made several flights due east to the Araguaia. These related the photos of Xingu to the co-ordinates of the rest of the charted world. A new map had been drawn.

Now that we were close to the site, Franklin worked out from the map and aerial photographs a point on the Xingu River directly east from the Centro Geographico. It was thus that, on the morning of the third day, we all stood at a place on the left bank of the Xingu with the knowledge that we were exactly due east and 17 km. 70 m. from the geographical centre of Brazil.

Raimundo and Clementi swung their machetes. Behind them, Franklin balanced a compass on a tripod and directed two men until the line from his compass pointed exactly west through the poles that they held. Gradually, the first dent in the foliage became a track that was littered with stumps and logs but which was a clear and straight line for the compass. Then, when 100 metres had been cut from the river, the distance was measured and a mark made on a tree. Each day, between four and ten of these marks would be chalked up, depending on the density of the jungle; each night, the cutting party would camp by the nearest stream. It was to go on for almost a month.

During this time the expedition was divided. There was always a team of seven men at the cutting head and those at the base camp varied from two to seven, depending on movements up and down the trail and on parties dispatched up-river to Claudio. Sometimes I carried food or messages up to the head, or went on a journey to the Juruna, but otherwise my duty became that of full-time hunter. The Brazilians were occupied on other jobs; the Indians were unreliable. Given ten bullets, it was impossible to tell whether Rauni, for instance, would shoot a brace of pig, sleep all day, or loose off the lot in a one-minute spasm of target practice.

Every morning, when first light drove the mosquitoes away, I would lean over and feel the gun beneath my hammock. To the amusement of the others, the Englishman took his responsibilities seriously. B.B. for a prowling puma would be changed to No. 5 shot for fowl. Then I would walk off, still sleepy, into the forest.

Within a few days, I realized that the animals I was hunting had never seen man before. From what I could gather from the Indians, their tribes seldom, if ever, ventured into this part of the forest. Wraithlike deer would pause ten paces away, wondering if I was as dangerous as a puma. Fowl, though nervous on the ground, seemed to feel secure twenty yards up in a tree. And tortoises strolled casually about the woods so that we built a pen for them at the base, where several could be kept at a time. In the tropics, meat has to be eaten within twenty-four hours; tortoises, like canned food, last for months.

For these reasons, five of six hours' work in the morning were usually enough to provide two meals a day. Then, after plucking and gutting, and eating and sleeping, my time was empty. There were few more interesting things to do than to go up to one of the Txukahamae warriors. He might be making a feathered head-dress or binding arrows. "Sit down," he would say. "I will teach you things. Then afterwards you will not be so ignorant."

This was Txukahamae country, this immense domain of forest about us, and to my eyes the two members of this tribe on our expedition, Rauni and Bebcuche, had recently seemed to grow in stature like wandering princes returned to their father's kingdom. For most of the time, one of them was with us at the base camp, and the other at the cutting head; if we met any Txukahamae, they were to shout warning of the flu epidemic. They also provided some measure of protection against the wild sections of the tribe that tend to kill strangers on sight. "I am a friend of the Txukahamae," Bebcuche taught me to say in his language. "I am brother of Rauni and Bebcuche. I am friend." As I was frequently in the forest alone and had heard a good deal about the Txukahamae attitude to strangers, I remembered this greeting with care.

Of all the contacted Indians in the region of Xingu, the Txukahamae are the most interesting. They lead a warring and nomadic life that is one of the most primitive in the world.

Their food consists of carrion, vultures, pumas, termites, insects, and the skin of the pig. They also—surprisingly—eat earth. They sleep on the ground—though other Indians have hammocks—and their huts are no more than banana leaves bent together on a fragile frame. Technically they are as far from the Xinguanos as those Indians are from the civilizados. They are so primitive that they do not have canoes, pots, musical instruments, or thatch huts; within the legend memory of the Juruna, they did not even possess a bow. Cultivation plays a minor part in the tribe's simple economy, and like the primitive aborigines of Australia and the bushmen of South Africa, the Txukahamae wander across the land feeding like scavengers on what they find and kill. Their nomad horde ranges over an enormous stretch of jungle, shuttling like the Mongols of Asia to and fro within self-imposed frontiers, slaughtering and plundering, as if inspired by the spirit of Genghis Khan. They have decimated the Juruna and the Suya to the south and slaughtered countless seringueiros to the north. The mere suspicion of their presence close to the Araguaia River ends all farming; telegrams are sent off for military help. The frontiers of the Txukahamae are wider than those of most European countries. Their home is the "robber camp" inland from the rapids of von Martius and three to four days' travel from our base at the Centro.

The word Txukahamae itself is the Juruna phrase for "the people who do not have a bow," but, in fact, the tribe is part of the Kayapo horde that has sway across the southern borders of Para. Amongst themselves they call each other by their two "clan" names—Mentuktire and Mekragnotire. The name Txukahamae only is used because the Villas contacted the tribe with the help of Juruna warriors.

"As we moved north into Xingu during the year 1946," Orlando once told me, "we heard about this tribe. A Kamayura chief just recently killed, the Juruna massacred, and then signs that the Txukahamae had made a reconnaissance close to our camp at Diauarum before they were scared by the dogs." Finally, near the rivers Manitsaua-Missu and Auaia-Missu, the Villas Boas found trails and camp sites belonging to the tribe and began to lay out presents in the slow process that leads up to the pacification of a primitive people.

In the summer of 1949, some Txukahamae—recognizable from the five-inch wooden disc in their lower lips —were seen on a sandbank but fled at the approach of the

Villas' canoe. "We found a camp, Adriano, and a trail that went along the bank of the river. We left some presents. Then we came back a few days later. There were tracks everywhere, so we knew that the Txukahamae had returned. Our presents were refused." Two months later, another investigation showed that the articles had been taken, and so some knives and half a dozen fishing lines were laid out in their place. "We also made the Juruna put down arrows and headdresses in a sign of friendship though at first they did not want to do so."

More months went by and then in the following year, alien smoke was seen close to the Juruna village. Whilst most of the tribe retreated to the safety of a sandbank in mid-stream, a reconnaissance with the Villas revealed a fresh camp nearby. More presents were placed.

Two years later, in the incredibly slow process of softening hostility in the primitive mind, the Txukahamae entered the Juruna village for the first time in peace. On this momentous occasion they exchanged some arrows for knives and tools left there by the Villas. "We went there," Bebcuche later told me, "many moons back when I was a boy. We gave arrows and the Juruna give knives, beads for ears, and water from the canoe." (He meant casiri which is alcoholic and too potent for the teetotal Txukahamae.) "This water," he said sadly, "is not a friend of the Txukahamae. Afterwards, all Txukahamae sick for many days."

Soon after this incident, the Villas returned and, calculating the route the nomads would have to take across the Auaia-Missu River, found a driftwood raft and inland from it a trail leading to a freshly abandoned camp. Once again, presents were left.

Then in 1953, at the site of an old Juruna village destroyed by the Txukahamae, Claudio and Orlando sensed

Indians in the forest around. They called. Their call was answered; a group of forty warriors came to the river bank armed with bows. In that moment of indecision, when the Txukahamae were ready to shoot but were watching what the others would do, the Juruna refused to cross. The brothers paddled over alone. They moved slowly towards that hostile, unmoving, unpredictable group of savages in some of the tensest few minutes of their career. "As I stepped out of the canoe," said Claudio, "I unbuckled my belt so that the revolver dropped into the water." Presents were given, and the Txukahamae visibly shook with trembling at the violent psychological shock of this first contact with civilizados. Suddenly, the strain became too great, and forty armed men turned and stampeded into the forest.

Later that year, another similar meeting was a success, and finally, in November, the village was visited. In exchange, some Txukahamae were taken to the post at Capitao Vasconcelos, and there I met Rauni and Bebcuche who were brothers of Krumare, leader of one of the clans. They had been there four to five months, spoke a smattering of Portuguese, and accepted the presents I gave them on arrival. A shirt, a mouth organ, and a coloured torch for Bebcuche; for Rauni, twelve bottles of highly scented hair oil. "Oileo," he muttered with pleasure. "Oileo to make Rauni beautiful." And he scuttled off to hide it in his private treasure horde of civilizado goods.

For some weeks after this first move, the relationship progressed no further. The Txukahamae did what Orlando asked about the hut and when lunch-time's rice arrived apologetically on the table a soggy and glutinous mass, I knew that one of them had tried his hand at cooking. Otherwise, though they lived and worked in the same building, they remained isolated and aloof.

One day, however, Rauni thrust his great caveman face into mine.

"What that?"[1] He pointed at the wrist compass I used when hunting.

Without thinking very much and knowing that the other Indians played on the Txukahamae's credulity, I said, "It points to the Txukahamae."

"It point to my village?"

"Yes. See the arrow. It is looking for the Txukahamae." (The main village is almost due north from Vasconcelos.)

"Hmmm," Rauni was suspicious. "Hmmm. Why you want machine for finding Txukahamae?"

"All the Migeles have them. They like Txukahamae—to eat. The Migeles eat many."

Rauni shook with laughter, great stormy gusts of mirth that would be incomprehensible to anyone outside the simple world of the Indian. He rolled on the floor and scooted around in the dust. He went to tell Bebcuche, and rattled his lip disc up and down as though it was an Alpine cow clapper. Finally he put both bear-like arms around me and pushed his beaming face close to mine.

"I eat you too," he said. "Txukahamae like Migeles."

Evidently a penetrating and enduring compliment had been paid by each of us, and in the days to come, whenever I met Rauni, he would take out his knife, beam, and sharpen it. "I have hunger today," he would say.

Once I cemented the joke by creeping up quietly behind the sleeping Indian. I put the post's largest pressure cooker beneath his hammock. "Rauni," I called, "will you please just step in over here."

For several minutes, the Txukahamae was quite helpless

[1] Txukahamae speech is very crude. It has only been partially softened in this and the following chapters for reasons given in the Author's Note at the beginning of the book.

with laughter, tears running down his lip disc, mixing with saliva, and then cascading over the edge in a waterfall to the ground.

By such playful and kindergarten means, a tenuous bridge of understanding was thrown across the chasm between the civilizado and the Indian.

Of the two Txukahamae, Rauni was the younger, about eighteen, with broad shoulders and standing some five feet nine inches in height. His long tresses hung back over his shoulders, bead necklaces dangled from his ear lobes, and ever since childhood his lower lip had been extended by bigger and bigger pieces of wood till, by my measuring, it had become the length of one and a half cigarettes across. Occasionally, this disc would fall out when he was in the river, and I would be obliged to swim around with goggles and flippers till it was found again. He was quick to learn, jovial, keen to talk once some friendship had been established, and very much a back-slapping, "I'll have a half pint of bitter" sort of person. He was, however, basically unreliable, selfish, and without shame as he used his charm to extract presents from the visiting pilots and air-crews.

Bebcuche, on the other hand, was seven or eight years older, and the reverse of almost every trait to be found in his half-brother. Where Rauni's face was smooth and comparatively handsome, his seemed beaten, anthropoid, and rather menacing in its structure. And where Rauni had a lip disc, he just had a hole under his mouth where the lower lip had burst. Bebcuche spoke only a few guttural words of Portuguese, was slow to learn, and had none of the jovial inquisitiveness that made Rauni such an amusing companion. He stood aloof; he looked ugly and sombre; he seldom talked to anyone who was not already a friend. But, over the months it was to become obvious that he was loyal, unselfish, gentle by nature, and thoughtful in the interests of the Villas and the expedition. After killing in the forest, Rauni was inclined to eat the game before he returned; Bebcuche hunted for the camp. Rauni would sulk and storm at the delays of the expedition and threaten to disappear into the jungle; Bebcuche just carried on with whatever he had been asked to do. He was neither a clever nor an amusing man, but an Indian of immense dignity. He could stand beside the Umslopogaas of Rider Haggard or the Chingachgook of Fenimore Cooper and rank as staunch in reality as they were in fiction.

In the evenings at Vasconcelos, one or both of the Txukahamae had often come to sit beside my hammock. Sometimes they talked, but usually they sang, for once Rauni had asked me "to do a Migeles song," and I had tried my best with "God Save the King." "The Migeles," Rauni had said with compassion, "cannot sing," and from then on he made a point of entertaining me with the highly developed voice and musical ear that is the Txukahamae's main pleasure in life.

"The Txukahamae sing," he would say, "when the sun is behind the trees, when the sun is high in the sky, and when the sun goes away to sleep. Then they sing all night."

"The women too?"

"The women, and the children, and the men. You will hear when you come to my village and live with us. We will sing for you."

"What do you sing about? Do you sing about hunting, and war, and about when you have eaten a big tapir and feel sleepy afterwards."

"Yes," said Rauni. "We sing about hunting and war and many other things. The song for mandioca. The song for making arrows. The song for walking home after taking honey. The song of corn. The song of the puma." And spitting across his disc, he would begin a low chant so that all the other Indians would gather around and say "beautiful," when he had finished. It was. Though the Txukahamae are primitive in other things, their musical sense is highly developed, and Rauni only needed to hear a Caraiba song once to be able to sing it again.

Thus, before the expedition set out, Rauni and Bebcuche had offered me something approaching friendship. They had often told me what we would do when we entered their country.

"Will you come hunting with me when you come to my land?"

"Of course. Are there many things to hunt?"

"Many!"

"Many?"

"Yes. Many. Deer. Tapirs and pumas. Pumas hunt Txukahamae. They like Txukahamae. They eat them."

"And the Txukahamae hunt the puma?"

"Yes. They hunt the puma. The black puma too. You come with me in my land and I show you. Now I have .22, I kill many pumas."

In Rauni's limited vocabulary the word "planting" had many uses.

"I go plant you Adriano in Txukahamae with rice and radio. We no have radio in Txukahamae. I like a radio and I plant in field. But I plant you straight up, like this." Rauni would stand up straight. "Your arms out. One vulture will sit on this arm, another on that arm."

"And an eagle on my head, Rauni?"

"Yes, an eagle on your head, with little eagles on your hands. Then I will come and talk to you. Down by the Xingu where before was the plantation of the Juruna a long time ago."

And now we were at the base camp and close to the place where all these things were to happen. This was the "Cuiaba" of the Txukahamae. One day Bebcuche and Rauni drew it for me in the sand.

All the afternoon we spent seated on our banana leaves smacking at the piumes and I noticed that Indian maps are very accurate about direction, though faulty with regard to distance. I also noticed that all places outside the Txuka-hamae village, and all places pinpointed in the forest during this talk, related to some battle or massacre.

To the east there was the story of Rauni at the Green Forest. As I was particularly interested in the Indian attitude to death and warfare, I persuaded him to tell me about it.

"I went," he told me, "I went to the other water over there [the Araguaia River] and I see horse. I never see horse before. I have much hunger, so I go to kill. But a Caraiba comes and takes machete in his hand. "Come here," he calls. Rauni wrinkled his face into a pompous and angry frown. "He very angry and want to kill me," he explained. "So I go away and break a stick for war-club. I run back and the Caraiba calls, 'Come here.' So I throw stick. He goes like this," Rauni pretended to duck, "and stick only hits hat. So I run away. But there I see a big dog. So I go break another stick and come to kill dog. I beat, but dog runs. Then I see horse again and I go with stick and beat. Adriano, do you know horses are very, very strong?" Some of the original surprise was still in Rauni's voice. "I beat here"—he indicated the back—"but horse runs. Afterwards, the Caraiba comes very angry. I break another stick and throw. But stick only hits Caraiba hair," Rauni concluded sadly, "and I have fear and run."

"Did the Caraiba die?"

"No. He alive, but has fear too. I run and there is no forest, only plain. I run and am very tired. When I come to a lake, I sleep, and afterwards three others come."

"Caraiba?"

"No. Txukahamae. They say to me, did the Caraiba kill you, and I say no. Then we go away together."

At this point Rauni left us, and Bebcuche described the story for me again with the map. I learned that the Txukahamae's visit to this pioneer fringe some fortnight's travel away had not been as innocent as Rauni had made it sound.

"Rauni go to kill and carry back carbine, machete, knife, and clothes. He go with Mengrire and Krumare, who already killed two," Bebcuche held up three fingers. (Despite much trying, he never learned to count.) "Mengrire, much time back, go to the Green Forest and see women working clothes in water near man with carbine. Man runs and has much fear. Krumare comes near and man . . ." Bebcuche enacted a man crouching and making croaking noises with his arms sheltering his head. His ghoulish face put on an expression of pathetic terror. "Krumare beat with war-club. Dead. Mengrire slaughter women. They carry to Txukahamae, carbine, knife, machete, and much clothes."

A repetition of this success had been the purpose of Rauni's visit.

To the east, I knew the Txukahamae preyed on the pioneer fringe of the Green Forest. To the south I was already aware that they had carried out large-scale massacres of the Juruna and Suya and minor brushes with the Indians around Vasconcelos. What happened over to the west, I learned when I turned the talk to medicine.

Bebcuche had just told me how the Txukahamae cast "medicine" (magic spells) to make civilizados fall asleep before an attack.

"Do you have medicine against Indians too?" I asked.

"We have. Much time ago when Txukahamae many, we go the-e-e-ere lo-o-o-ng." He pointed to the west and drew out his words to express distance. "We come like this"—he made a crescent movement with his hands—"and all the tribe Kreen-Akarore asleep. We work medicine and then when morning come, we work arrow and rifle. Fire. Fire. Fire. Bang. Bang. Bang. Kreen-Akarore do arrow, arrow, too. Then chief of Kreen-Akarore, string of his bow breaks. He runs. Others run. Three dead." Bebcuche held up four fingers.

"Then much time more and we see chief of Kreen-Akarore passing in forest. We kill chief and take son."

Bebcuche continued with an almost incomprehensible account of a series of dog fights in the forest in which one or two men were killed each time. The tribe Kreen-Akarore have never been seen by civilizados, but Bebcuche indicated their giant height by holding up his hands above his head and jumping. He said their biceps were as big as thighs and their bows as thick as a man's wrist. He also said that Mengrire, a boy captured from them some years before, was below average height, though according to Orlando he measured six feet two inches or more.

One incident in the war with this "giant" tribe Bebcuche described like this:

"Then Kreen-Akarore come and only one Txukahamae there. This Txukahamae in plantation, only one man with one woman. Man fires rifle. Then runs. Woman can't run. She has sick leg. She walk like this." Bebcuche walked across the clearing on his hands and bottom like a legless cripple. "Then many Txukahamae run from the village and Kreen-Akarore kill mother of my mother and her brother. Then afterwards Txukahamae savage and go, long, long, lo-o-ong, and kill Kreen-Akarore and break all bones."

"How many did they kill?"

"One."

"Did you break bones after he was dead?"

"Yes."

"Why after he was dead, Bebcuche?"

"Txukahamae savage. Kreen-Akarore kill many Txukahamae. I break bones. I boy," Bebcuche showed by the height
of his hands above the ground that he had been about eleven
years old. "I cry much, cry and cry when they kill the mother
of my mother. I beat. I beat. I beat. I break many bones.
Beat. Beat. Beat. BEAT."

A fierce violence came into Bebcuche's voice and it
would have been easy to say that brutality was the over-riding
mark of his character. And yet I knew that, in other ways, this
man was a friendly, gentle person with a strong love of life.

"Adriano, you have fear of death?" he had asked once
when I survived a risky moment out hunting.

"Yes."

"I too. Very much."

"Why Bebcuche?"

"Because when die, I finish." His face was soft and his
eyes sad.

"Don't you go up above into the sky?" I asked.

"I don't know. Do Caraiba?"

"I don't know, Bebcuche."

And yet again, to add once more to the strange contrasts
of this primitive mind, Bebcuche himself had killed entirely without point. One of the dangers for civilizados who
try to help a dying, primitive race is that they tend to
idealize their charges into a sweet and noble people whose
only fault is their inability to avoid an unjust fate. Love
grows in their hearts, and though they try to control it in the
interests of science and a cool judgment, soon their people
have no blemish in their eyes and can do no wrong. Perhaps I was slipping into this state of mind myself. But
later that night Bebcuche jolted me violently into the world
of truth where good and evil live side by side within the soul
of a single man. "When we come to my village," he remarked casually, "Orlando gives a new gun to me."

"You'll have two guns then."

"Yes. I will have two guns, and when I get back to my village if anyone plays savage with me. I kill. Bang."

"That's nice," I said absently. "Have you killed many people, Bebcuche?"

Ki-i-i-ill. Sla-a-ay." The words were deep and long. "I kill three."

It seemed that he and two others had come across six Xavante women and children in the forest and Bebcuche had clubbed one woman and dashed the brains out of two children.

"Did you take many guns or clothes from them?"

"No, only one knife."

"Then why did you kill?"

"We don't know them. First time we see."

It had been as pointless as that.

There our conversation ended. The sky threatened to rain, and I ran out from the hut to untie my hammock from its place between the trees.

The battery radio was bringing a faint reminder of another existence into the enormous quiet of primeval forest. "Toddy is the ideal drink," it said. "Toddy is delicious. Nutritious. A tin of Toddy is an investment in health. Toddy before bed. Toddy in the morning. Toddy for the children. Toddy. Toddy. Toddy. TODDY. TODDY."

Orlando was in his hammock reading by candlelight a cheaply printed edition of Edgar Wallace's The Scarlet Circle. Dilton was fiddling with a torch; Sergio was trying to skin an animal like a ferret; and outside the forest rustled busily as if all the trees in thousands of square miles of empty land were queuing up to peer at us. Very soon I was dropping off to sleep on the ground not far from Bebcuche.

"Rain not friend of Migeles man," he murmured sympathetically. Then, as was his custom, he continued talking to himself in Txukahamae.

15

WHY THE PUMA KILLS

IN XINGU THE rainy season lasts from December to the end of April. Occasionally, the rain stops for a few hours, and sometimes there is a break of several days or more. Otherwise, the water falls in deluge beyond all European imagination. Great plains, like the land between Vasconcelos and the Kuluene, are nine feet under water. The sandbanks disappear, and the rivers seem to become the land itself, spreading for miles beyond their confines and tearing down the trees in the forest. The animals flee to the islands; the Indians go hungry because it is difficult to move; and the mosquitoes are crazy with hunger.

Then in May the water stops, and within a month the moisture has run off the sandy soil, the forest has dried, and the Indians creep out to watch the sun polish golden sandbanks out of the river. This is the good time in Xingu, and its final month—September—served us well at the outset of the Centro Geographico expedition. The skies were blue. For thirty days there was not a cloud.

Then, in the first week of October, black puffs began to

appear from the direction of the Atlantic and passed over us en route for the Andes. A huge rampart of cloud slowly piled up, dark and tall, in the eastern part of the sky, and though reconnaissance puffs went by, the rampart held back, daily becoming bigger and more menacing, every morning seeming to lean closer over and above us. We had been five months without rain, and Orlando said that this was the hurricane that would change the season. Every year it brought a power of storm and gale that was not felt again till the same time twelve months later. Bebcuche told me "the sky will shout and send down long fire to kill Indians." After this storm, and for the rest of the expedition, we would have sharp squalls of twenty minutes or more several times a day till the rains broke properly in December, but this first typhoon was the great violence in the calendar of Xingu. It was the executioner of Amazonia. The forest, rotten from five months of easy living, would be torn apart. All of us in the camp waited tensely for that looming eastern dam to break.

It is in this season that the panthers choose to mate. In general, the South American "cat," more accurately known as the puma, leaves man alone, but at the month of the first rain, deep coughing noises can be heard in the forest and the Indians say that this is made by two or three pumas following a female and offering their suit. As the courting sometimes goes on for days and the male will not leave the female with a rival, the "cats" go hungry. They become desperate and fearless in their need to kill.

Roughly at this time, Bebcuche's dog, Robar, staggered into the camp with great bite marks through his neck into the lower jaw and also above the eye into his head; the puma must have sprung from behind and slightly to the right, making one bite before the dog managed to tear itself away.

After this, a curiously neat chain of events led up to the ambush.

One day, when the storm was still building, I returned from hunting to find Bebcuche sitting in my canoe. "Puma hungry for Txukahamae," he explained. He told how he had walked down the bank with a bow, fishing for tucanare, and how by chance he had doubled back on his tracks to see fresh puma footprints close behind his own. He had crept forward to wait for me and my gun in the canoe. That night Bebcuche had a complex about pumas.

When I came quietly into the base camp after a brief but necessary excursion into the forest, I found myself looking down the barrel of his .24 bore. "Why you make noise like puma walking?" he asked indignantly. Then, seeing my surprise: "I hear puma talking near." He surrounded our hammocks with dry banana leaves so that an approach during the night would wake us from our sleep.

Next morning, I went up the track carrying fish and game for the people at the cutting head. I also had some radio news for Orlando; a friend of his who supported the National Park had come to power in the elections of the State of São Paulo.

About two to three hours out, my eyes were caught by a flash of white on the trail to the left, and, peering through a dense thicket of bushes, I gradually made out a white and faintly moving breast. At that shoulder level, it should have been a crested mutum; I fired. But when eventually I forced my way through the bushes, I found an enormous eaglelike bird with a wing span that must have been six feet or more. It was gorgeous with glistening white plumes. A king vulture. These are rare in Xingu but can be seen more often on the cattle lands to the north, where the vampire bat incises the skin of cattle during the night and laps the blood that flows from the wound. In this way paralytic rabies is passed from the bat to the steer, which then staggers about the plain watched by a group of vultures till it collapses to die on the ground. The vultures descend, and then a king slowly floats down to the carrion, dropping slightly to one side of the earlier birds as they fight and tear the steer to pieces. The king, white and regal, advances. The subjects, black and small, retire. He dines alone, sometimes working himself right into the belly of the beast so that he emerges gory from head to foot. This, however, was the first time I had seen a king vulture so close, and I was surprised by the contrast between the pure white of its feathers and the upper half of its body. The head and neck were completely bald, and though clean and bright in sheen, were vivid in the orange, purple, and scarlet colours of putrifying flesh. It meant death. It was one of the most disgusting things I had seen in the forest. I felt as though I was going to be sick.

Close by was the reason for the king's presence—the freshly killed remains of a medium-sized sururucu. Large specimens of this snake can reach six feet in length, with the head as thick as a man's leg and with a bite that is the most lethal in the forest. It is the only Amazonian snake which will attack man without provocation, and caboclos say that it can run at the speed of a deer. Sergio, I learned later, had stumbled on to it during the night when moving on the trail by the light of a torch. He had fired—just in time.

On the morning after my journey there was no need to hunt, and as 12-bore cartridges were running low, I decided to experiment with a .20-bore that one of the others had lent me.

It was dawn when I set out.

Downstream from the base camp, where Bebcuche had been two days before, there was a long gully that ran parallel to the river and made easy walking. Along it I picked my way carelessly, over-confident from months of

hunting in the forest. I paid more attention to my shoes—
they were falling apart despite their binding of lianas—than
to the jungle around. I twisted and turned and bent through
the bushes to avoid more tears in my tattered shirt. Around
my waist the leather strap from a binocular case held up
my trousers, while cartridges flopped loosely in the only
pocket remaining to my jeans.

Every now and again I would move over to the right to
peep like a rabbit through the foliage out across the water at
the black parapet that was holding back the sun in the east.
Wind brought waves to the river, pushing them against the
shore, and the trees were heaving and groaning slightly in the
earth. The birds were strangely quiet, and the huge looming
storm sat out on the other side of the water, almost tipping
over at forty-five degrees in its leaning towards us. The dam
was about to break.

Not long after, I heard a series of startled grunts, like a
man snorting through the nose, which meant that a "sounder"
of caititu (small forest pig) was close by. They were moving
and milling about on the other side of an impenetrable fence
of thorn bush about fifty yards away and almost certainly
could not have noticed my presence upwind. It was a warning. It did not register. Twenty-bore cartridges loaded with
bird shot are not suitable for pig hunting, and so I passed on
and was soon stalking a group of jacubim fowl sitting high
in a line of trees. These were some of the tallest trees I had
seen in Xingu; the lowest of their branches were thirty
yards or more above the ground.

I fired. The bird flapped idly away. A few minutes later,
I fired again. Another bird departed. A third shot was
equally useless. At the fourth—gunfire marking my passage
up the gully—I decided that either the cartridges were not
strong enough to penetrate the wing at that range, or the
poor fit of the gun stock was putting me off. I looked about for

a place to aim and test the gun. Suddenly by some miracle of apprehension or undeserved warning from God, I sensed two lithe golden bounds, so swift that they only flickered at the retina on the corner of my eye. I screamed; it was quite instinctive. Then there was a third bound, and the puma was one split second from his leap on to my shoulder. I screamed again, this time remembering it was precisely what I should do.

Though I had started to whirl the gun round at the first sense of danger, the puma was so swift that by the time I had made the 180-degree turn, he had been startled to a position almost ten yards away.

The puma had obviously decided that I was not a new mark of pig. Caititu and boars make different noises. He was wondering what to do.

I wondered too. There he was, standing a dozen paces from me, bigger than the biggest dog I have ever seen, but not as large as a jaguar or full-grown leopard. Otherwise, the only thing that my mind took in was his light brown colouring and the motionless stance as though he were stuffed. I knew—from description—that this was what the Brazilians call a tawny puma and that he was therefore smaller than the black or spotted big cats. By tradition he is, however, the most "valiant" of his kind, being inquisitive, unpredictable, and usually spoiling for a fight.

We stood without movement for several minutes whilst my brain refused to work. Pumas seldom run from man because they are the masters of their world. This one, never having seen a man before, was in all probability even less inclined to yield. My first thought was to creep away. But retreat was impossible. The river was behind, and movement to either right or left gave the puma the chance to stalk me, hidden by one bank of the gully. On the other hand, if I chose to fire at his heart and the little pellets missed that vital organ, I had a wounded puma, the most vicious thing in the forest, on my more than shaky hands.

"It's easy to kill the puma," the Indians told me later. Apparently having survived the first onslaught, I was perfectly safe. Face to face, the puma will only come forward slowly, pawing almost playfully at the ground. He will not repeat the windlike speed of his first sally. Since his other forest adversaries fight with a leap or charge, the cat is invariably surprised by the killing reach of a war-club held outstretched in a man's arm. If I had not killed with the shot, I could still have swung with my gun. "Hit puma on nose. Boomph. Nose soft. Gun hard. Puma sleep." Bebcuche explained it all later.

But at the time, I decided to shoot at the face. If I blinded the cat with pain, perhaps he would go away.

I raised the gun to my shoulder. He did not seem put out by the movement. I squinted down the ball sight. He was not embarrassed by my interested stare. I pulled the trigger. He was—quite suddenly—gone.

It took me about forty seconds to force the damp cartridge out of the breech with the machete. Then I crept along the bank, looking nervously about me, until a minute or two later I heard a series of hoarse screams strangely like those of a man in the extremity of agony. They were in the forest over to my right, and the animal seemed to be moving south and west.

I hurried back to the camp and returned with my 12-bore loaded with B.B. in the hope of putting the animal out of its pain. I was accompanied by Bebcuche, who padded about looking at the tracks. Apparently the puma had been stalking the pig and, oblivious to all the signs of his passage, I had almost blundered into him.

We searched for roughly an hour and then, quite suddenly, the dam in the heavens broke. The hurricane exploded over the forest, and the dome of branches above our heads—until then as solid as St. Paul's—writhed so that we appeared to be upside down and shaking in an earthquake. Untried for five months, the rotten trees began to crash to the ground, branches, leaves, whole tree trunks exploding in a mass of rocketing splinters and flailing lianas. It was like an air raid with shattered skyscrapers tumbling about us. Day became night, and then the lightning made it day again with a vast battery of explosive illumination. First we would see one part of the sky burst into light between the foliage and then, in chain reaction, all the clouds across the heavens. Huge blocks of wood burst at our feet; lianas slashed and writhed as if they were flailing hawsers. Like soldiers on a battlefield, we took our chance through the barrage, and hurried back to camp.

There the others had been fighting desperately to save the boats as tidal waves swept across the water and hurled themselves at the canoes. The tree trunk next to my hammock had crashed in wreckage only one or two yards away. And now, the rain. It came with a violence suited to the great elemental forest of Xingu. The roof of banana leaves gave way; the floor became a river, the walls a vent for the howling waterfall. The fire went out, liquid swilled about in the next meal's abandoned meat and rice. People shivered in groups and turned in towards each other, trying to ignore what was around and under and above. "Rain of the devil!" one of the caboclos shrieked. "Rain of abandoned morals and parentage. Rain of . . ."

I crouched not far from Bebcuche beneath what was left of the flimsy banana-leaf shelter and waited for the storm to pass. I had been offered a puma on a plate and what had I done? "So Adriano only plays with the puma," Bebcuche said. "Adriano plays like a child," he roared, elaborating the joke to himself over and over again. The Indian habit of repetition can be tedious on occasion.

"Why, Bebcuche"—I had heard the story before, but it would change the subject—"why was the puma angry?"

"You don't understand, no?"

"No, I don't understand, Bebcuche."

"Then I tell you, so afterwards you do understand."

He launched into his story. Like so many of the Txukahamae legends it began at the beginning "much, much time ago, when the Indians live in the sky." Apparently one of these Indians had found a hole dug by an armadillo and through it had seen the green plains and trees of the jungle beneath.

"Txukahamae make string like I show you with lianas, and many Txukahamae climb down to the jungle with their wives, and children, and grandfathers. Then savage Indian cut string and Txukahamae no have string to go back. They stay here. At this time, much, much time ago, Txukahamae no have fire." Bebcuche paused to stress the animal-like poverty of this life.

"Then, when the sons of these men already a long time dead, one Txukahamae Indian go into the forest with his beautiful woman and passes one, two, three, four, five moons with her. Then brother-in-law comes and says, 'You want macaw for head-dress?'

" 'Yes,' the Indian says, 'I want macaw to make me beautiful.'

" 'Then you come with me,' and brother-in-law put tree [Bebcuche meant a sapling with branches cut to act as a ladder] to this cliff and Indian climbs up and catches macaw.

" 'Throw down macaw to me,' says brother-in-law.

" 'No,' says Indian, and throws a rock that beats brother-in-law on hand. Brother-in-law cries much and is angry and takes tree away so that the Indian can't come down.

"And now, Adriano, the Indian sits on the high place and becomes very thin till many days more a puma comes who has been hunting with bow and arrow and killed a tapir. He sees the Indian's shadow. He tries to catch it. He jumps once. He tries to catch it. He jumps twice. He puts the tapir down and looks up.

" 'Come down,' puma says. 'I have tapir for you to eat.'

"But the Indian has fear. 'I have fear of you,' he says.

" 'No, don't have fear,' puma says, 'I like you. Throw me your macaw.'

"The Indian throws macaw and the puma eats it. Now the Indian has more fear.

" 'Come down,' says puma. 'I like you.'

"So the Indian comes down and goes to the puma's house and the puma gives him deer and pig and tapir and ant-bear to eat. They have fire and the puma woman cooks at the fire.

"After one moon, puma woman says, 'I don't like you Indian. You eat deer and pig and tapir and ant-bear and don't work. You go away.'

"So the Indian goes to the puma when he comes from hunting and they swim together in the river and the Indian tells the puma that the puma woman is savage with him. Puma says, 'I don't like puma woman any more. You can kill her. You go into the forest and work bow.'

"So Indian works bow and one straight arrow and in the morning, when the puma has gone hunting, puma woman wakes up and is angry. 'You eat deer and pig and tapir and ant-bear and don't work' she says. Then Indian takes the bow and shoots puma woman deep in the chest. Then he makes a basket and puts deer and pig inside and goes back to his village.

Sirivi, one of the Juruna warriors who killed the seringueiros

Typical seringueiros transporting supplies on the outskirts of the forest

Claudio Villas Boas

Rauni the Txukahamae smoking a civilizado pipe. His lip-disc is four inches wide

Aligning the trace to the Centro

Cutting the post at the Geographical Center of Brazil

Claudio about to give an injection at the Txukahamae encampment

A Txukahamae hut is no more than a few banana leaves thrown onto a slender frame of branches

"Then Indian sleeps in his mother's house for one night, but afterwards he says to his mother, 'You Txukahamae woman, you have no fire. The puma woman has fire and it has much beautifulness. It makes me warm and it cooks the meat.' So he talks to the other Txukahamae, many men all together, and afterwards they all go to the puma house and steal the fire.

"Because of this," Bebcuche said, "the puma is angry."

16

THE LAST EL DORADO

DURING MOST OF September and October, the expedition
lived in the forest cutting at the Centro trail. Yard by yard
the trace moved towards the west, and every morning I
would hunt in a new direction looking for a lake or hill to
vary the monotony of tropical jungle. But the forest remained always the same, a dank squalor of vegetation that
yielded before our machetes and then grew at redoubled
pace beside and above and beneath us. The trees were as
enveloping as the air we lived in; the dripping of the foliage
was as incessant as traffic noises in a town. We seldom saw the
sun, we never escaped the mosquitoes, and, unlike conquistadors or explorers, no great objective stood before us
leading on to greater efforts. At the top of a mountain there
is a view for the mountaineer; for us at the Centro there
would be trees. Pizarro, Orellana, and Cortes had marched
in the hope that a dream would come true; our objective was
to trample on the last great legend of geography. Limply, we
proceeded with our task.

One night, as several of us were swinging in our hammocks, I thought about the meaning of our journey and how this planet earth has always contained remote, uncharted lands where man can locate his unworldly dreams. A few square inches that are blank on a map where lost cities, living dinosaurs, and mountains of gold can exist in imagination, and where—for all anyone knows—they may prove to be in fact. Our objective was to destroy this tradition. We were struggling in the forest to proclaim conquest over the largest of these remaining "white patches" and over the greatest of the dreams. Death to the jungle. Death to legend. Death—the word seemed to clatter about in the claustrophobic confines of the clearing—death to the last El Dorado.

I felt across my body for ticks; I had plucked off 168 that day, but the movement had become unconscious and my flow of thought tumbled idly on.

That night, it seemed that ever since Columbus and Henry the Navigator, men had conspired to ruin the playground that the earth had been for the mediæval dreamer. The glorious legend of Atlantis had exploded with Diaz, the North-West Passage with the men who followed Hudson. Captain James Cook had brought Terra Incognita Australis into factual dimensions, and after the era of Stanley and Livingstone you could no longer talk of the mines of Solomon or of Prester John. Year by year, the world had become increasingly a question of fact till even magic names like Samarkand and the forbidden city of Lhasa had ceased to be titles of romance. The earth had grown barren, till only one great realm of imagination remained. The Forest of Amazonia. The land of El Dorado.

Why, I wondered, had so much legend and dreaming been sited in this soul-destroying jungle? Because it was the most impenetrable large territory on earth? Maybe. Because nowhere else had Europeans found unimagined civilizations guarding stores of untold wealth? Probably. Cortes had captured Montezuma in a city of pyramid temples stained with the blood of human sacrifice. Pizarro had seen a stone-paved hall filled with the golden ransom of an Inca king. No wonder that Amazonia had become the home of legend and was for four centuries ransacked for El Dorado, the cousin of the Inca cities.

"Manoa, the Imperial City of Guiana, which the Spaniards call El Dorado, that for the greatness, for the riches, and for the excellent seat it far exceedeth any of the world." I muttered Raleigh's words out into the quiet of the trees. The Empire of the Muses. The Capital of the Omaguas. The town of the Amazons. Each was spoken slowly as befitted legend titles that had dragged ten thousand men to the grave. Ambrosio de Alfinger, Bartolome Sailler, Georg von Speier, Sebastian de Belalcazar, Nicholas Federmann, Philip von Huten, Pedro de Ursua, the Quesadas, Berrio, Nicholas Martinez, Vincente de la Fuente. There was a fine pirate ring about these leaders' names. Fawcett. Colonel Percy Harrison Fawcett. That, too, struck at the imagination—the last of the great dreamers who had gone searching for cities in the forest. He had come to this land of Xingu and his first objective, a stone tower, was marked on the map almost at the place of our camp. It had been 1925. At that time there were tracts of New Guinea, watersheds on the Venezuela-Guiana borders, and valleys in Yunan and Tibet that were still unknown, but these had only been small pieces of territory. Otherwise, the world of 1925 had been explored, except for Antarctica. Nowhere else on earth could have concealed a lost civilization but Xingu. And Fawcett had only emphasized the drama by disappearing himself.

But now, on the day that our machetes cut past the 17th km. and the 70th m., the Villas' fifteen-year journey would reach its climax. The last white patch would be defeated and the whole great tradition of dreaming would receive its public blow. The forest was about to be conquered, and there would be nowhere else in the world for the Fawcetts and the El Dorados. Unknown regions and lost tribes would still remain in Orlando's domain; but the purpose of our journey was to show that any of these places could be explored with a single expedition, that it was policy, not inability, that preserved the isolation of the Indian. By cutting our way to a spot chosen quite arbitrarily by mathematicians in Rio, we were demonstrating that the jungle could hold nothing back from the nation of Brazil. The Heart of Amazonia was about to die, and the great forest which had defied man longer than the Himalayas, the Antarctic, and the Sahara would, like the other three, become a vassal to civilization. The thought was not inspiring. I swung my hammock gently between the trees and a few minutes later fell asleep as the mosquitoes buzzed outside my net.

At midnight, the rain began to fall. We all moved into the hut and slept on the ground.

. . . .

It was just after lunch next day when Claudio Villas Boas arrived in the camp by the Centro Trail. He appeared quite unexpectedly, walking up from the river bank and looking very tired and worn. The journey from the Juruna village which had taken the main party two days with motors, he and two warriors had just done with paddles in two and a half. They had travelled all night.

Claudio's greeting was to seize and pluck the mutum I had just brought in. His chubby face was pale and very drawn.

"Things are bad, Adriano. The flu has spread to the Juruna."

Feathers flew with each of his statements.

"There are four pneumonia cases. One is coughing blood and I am worried. They need all the penicillin and Vitamin C that I can take back."

In half an hour the mutum was cooked and torn to pieces. Claudio and the two Juruna then set out on the return journey with medicines, an outboard motor, and Jorge the mechanic.

A few days later, Pioni, José, and I followed them in the aluminum boat. The Central Brazilian Foundation plane that had been missing so long had eventually flown down the course of the Xingu, sighted the mooring of our boats at the base camp, and dropped a message arranging a rendez-vous ten days ahead at Diauarum.

We had been sent upstream and, until our date with the plane, were to help Claudio with the Juruna.

It was a long and stormy journey. The wind was high and nearly tossed us out of the boat to the piranhas so that when we arrived in the village we were tired and dripping wet. I was conscious, however, that we had been travelling amongst the great things of nature—a powerful expanse of water, burning sands, limitless sky, and a land that had nobility in its emptiness and size. The squalor of Claudio's hovel of sickness could not have been a more depressing contrast. The hut was dismal and slung with filthy ham-mocks. An old stove made from a tin can cast a miserly light about the corners. The Kayabi lay in filthy hammocks in filthy clothes, sick and showing that they knew they were sick; all the animal vitality that usually made them such noble beings had utterly gone. Bows, firewood, pans, odd bits of food were scattered amongst the dirt on the floor.

Claudio came up to us looking very dirty and with his clothes hanging limply about his body. He seized with de-light upon the jacubim we had shot on the journey. "Good. This will do for lunch tomorrow."

I counted the people in the hut. One, two, . . . fifteen. A jacubim is no bigger than a hen.

Some time later, when we were all in our hammocks, Claudio told us that things had not been easy with most of the Juruna and Kayabi down with flu and no one to hunt or to canoe up to the plantations for food. He had moved the Kayabi from the Manitsaua-Missu into one hut and the Juruna were in the other three close by, but besides the daily tours with injections and Vitamin C he dared not relax his attention for a minute. Each of the pneumonia cases had passed the crisis, but at any time of night or day a fevered Indian might decide—against all warning—to cool his burning body in the river. Then it would start all over again.

For the next four days I hunted almost incessantly. It would rain all night and then we would set out in the wet-ness of a miserable dawn. Paddle. Paddle. Paddle. Not heavy thrusts at the water, as we had a long way to go, but a rounded swing that just missed my knees where they pro-jected over the shallow side of the canoe. My legs would be cramped in the narrow sloping bottom and behind would be Siriri, the Juruna warrior. We had been hunting together on my first visit to his village, and I knew him well.

One particular morning when we landed, Siriri took an axe to cut honey out of a wild bees' nest and I went after game, padding through the trees which were noisy with rain. The effect was similar to hunting in a smoke-screen. I couldn't hear the cry or movement of my prey; my quarry couldn't hear me. It was thus that I missed the biggest prize that I could have shot for the village, an animal for which I had once waited half a night slung in a hammock between branches forty feet above the ground—a tapir. As casually as two ships passing in a fog, I saw its huge shadow moving amongst the other shadows twenty yards away and, as it dis-appeared into the greyness, I fired in the desperate hope of cutting a ligament in the back of its leg. I failed. But later, Siriri struck a band of mutum. He got two and I six in an incredible chaos of shrieking birds and swift movement through the trees. Distributed around the village, they were a temporary solution to the problem of food.

By this time most of the Juruna were better, and the trouble mainly lay with the Kayabi. They disliked the Juruna, resented not being allowed to go back to their own village, and, having no understanding of the idea of contagion, could not appreciate why they had to stay. It was straining all Claudio's years of friendship to make them do what they considered both pointless and unpleasant.

At first his problem was to make feverish patients stay in their hammocks and keep warm, instead of hunting and fishing in the rain. But now that they had acquired the idea of their own sickness, nothing would induce them to help themselves. They picked ticks quietly from each other's hair and lay, two to their double hammocks, heads sticking out of a vent in the cloth each side, giving a quaint impression, in that Indian hut, of steam baths made for two. Several were convalescent, but it was still we who had to do the cooking. Jorge, the mechanic, spent three or four hours a day pounding Indian corn into a fine dust. When this was stewed with water, it made an insipid but digestible porridge. The Kayabi did not offer to help, and it would have been unwise to order them to do so.

Claudio told me that epidemics were unusually destructive in Xingu because the civilizado had to work against the patient. Without supervision, the sick took no rest, ate no food, and spat out medicine as soon as the doctor's back was turned. Only injections—painful and involving a fussy process of sterilization and manipulation—were appreciated, as a magic that was both interesting and powerful. As it was, all of us could feel the resentment creeping across the hut's filthy floor, licking over boxes, sliding round hammocks, and curling about our part of the building. The Kayabi were sick, they were weary for their home, and though they must have comprehended in some way that we were working for their good, they displayed a child's disobedience to everything its nanny does.

It even began to affect Claudio. "Out of your hammock," he said to a warrior one morning. "Because you were ill days ago is no reason why you can't take two paces to get your own food now. Oh, Kayabi, my son, do you expect me to feed you like your mother?"

And then turning to us: "My people. Oh, my people. What a trial my people are." His words might have sounded histrionic anywhere else. But not in that hut with its strange resentment seeping like a poison gas across the chasm of noncomprehension between our two civilizations. Claudio was doing something in the nature of a Florence Nightingale, and I could have agreed with some of the Indians' feelings if he had displayed goodness on his face and was convinced of the divine right of his doing. We are always grateful to the charitable, but deep inside, concealed by all our superstructure of Christianity and civilization, we hate their saintliness. But this man, so plump and dirty, with clothes hanging about him, so unimpressive in the squalor, hopeless, knowing in despair that if he saved a life now it would probably, in a few years' time, be lost for some reason attributable to his own work, asking not for recognition nor even help . . . nothing inside me could have hated him. But perhaps for the Indian it was different. Previously, he had been proud as the king of his forest. Now he owed his life to a stranger. It was a bitter thing to swallow.

On our part, we lived silent and brusque lives in an atmosphere of despair. We knew that with our assistance the Kayabi would be unlikely to die, but it was like patching up an unsuccessful suicide who is determined to kill himself once he is better. The resentment and misunderstanding was deeper than the disease. It seemed to portray for us the whole problem of the dying Indian race. We desperately wanted to help and yet knew that our task was almost certainly one of complete futility. And thus, like doctors in a plague hospital, our minds kept strictly to the practical details of duty. It was an arid life. Work and a wooden face. Angry young men and emotional tirades can only be afforded by a situation of hope.

Some days later the epidemic was almost over, and Claudio decided that he would set out next morning to mark out a landing line for the aeroplane on a sandbank near to the Centro. The rest of us were to wait for a day before going up to Diauarum to notify the pilot of this new change in plan.

On the night before we separated, I brought in several jungle fowl. "I killed one, Claudio, especially for you. It's to eat on the journey." I deeply respected and liked him for his crusade with the Indians, and it was one of the few things I could do to help.

"No, no, Adriano. Keep it here. You will need it yourselves."

"Heavens, Claudio. You can't go off for several days in unknown jungle without food. What are you going to eat on the journey?"

It was a stupid thing to say.

"Food? What do I need food for? There is food in the forest. I have two Indians who can fish and my revolver. Poosha. Once I walked for twenty-eight days with only a .22. And on my trail we are often short of food. José [not the expedition's José] is the only man who hasn't fainted from hunger. All others have collapsed. It's a hard life for the

men on my road. When it rains, it vomits. We carry sixty
pounds on our back up the track to where the cutting is done.
Then no dinner. And rain, my God, what rain! It pours all
night and nowhere shelter. Not even a bamboo-leaf hut,
because there hasn't been time. Then no breakfast, and
work on the road in the mud. Men die. One had terrible
pains in the stomach, but before we could get medicine from
the base, he was dead. It's a terrible life and there is no na-
tionalistic ideal as in war to help you bear it.

"In the rains, when the planes can't land, I have had food
parachuted in. But I don't like to do it. The Air Force is an
Air Force, not a grocery service. Often I have only three men
on the trail and four men out hunting. Hunting all day. The
men say they can't work with too much hunger. They need
coffee in the morning or they collapse with dizziness. Look
at Clementi. Probably the best man I have on the trail, but
without food for two days he is useless. Every man is different, and you have to learn his faults and advantages. I,
for instance, don't need food. I can go for days without it."

The pale, chubby little man went on, and I reflected that
acts of extreme endurance must in some way be the product
of pride in oneself, and that though Claudio was a humble
man one should not trample too casually on that hard
backbone which makes endurance possible.

Eventually it all smoothed out, and we stewed the bird
and then added rice to cook with the gravy. He and two
Juruna left with this pan of food next morning, and on the
day after, Pioni, José, and I took the aluminum boat up to
Diauarum. We made the rendezvous with the plane,
told the pilot about landing on the sandbank, and watched
him take off again, heading towards the north.

We waited throughout the afternoon, increasingly anxious about the pilot's fate. Then, when twenty-four hours had

passed and the plane had still not returned, we realized there must have been an accident and set out to look for the crash.

The hours passed, the outboard motor sputtered and hummed, and we peered gloomily at the jungle on either side of the river.

Eventually our boat arrived at the Juruna village. As we were wondering whether we could afford to give the by-then convalescent Kayabi a tow in their canoes part of the way up the Manitsaua-Missu, we heard the sound of an aeroplane passing to the east.

"The pilot," José said, "must have damaged his under-carriage on landing. Now he's repaired it and is on his way home."

The Juruna cheered. The sun came out from behind a cloud, and, suddenly, everything seemed to be under con-trol. Not one life had been lost in the epidemic; the plane was safe.

And then, the noise of the engines reminded us. The pilot had said in his few minutes at Diauarum that there was another flu outbreak at Vasconcelos and that the labour-ers there were almost in despair. Amongst those already dead were an Aweti and the chief of the Kuikuro.

. . . .

On October 14, nothing very much happened, except that two weary-looking men cut past the seventieth metre of the seventeenth kilometre. It was the Centro Geographico. They sighed with relief, for they had great blisters on their hands. There was nothing to see but trees.

At the time, I happened to be travelling on the river, returning to the Juruna village, but I learned later that the cutting team gathered in the humid atmosphere to discuss their success. They gazed listlessly at the trees and vegetation that they had worked so long to see, and Orlando talked about the particularly dense quality of the jungle. A small group could not hope to cut a 1,000 metre airstrip in such terrain and he decided to make a clearing 100 m. x 50 m. That would leave a mark visible from the air for five years or more. Then the expedition would have to burn an airstrip on a large plain discovered by the aeroplane fifty kilometres to the north. This could be used for a base for a later full-scale clearance team.

Wearily, the party went back to work. Two days were spent cutting the clearing so that only an enormous jatoba tree was left standing just to the right of the centre. To this, various odd pieces of tin from the camp were nailed, and nearby a stake was driven into the ground mentioning that this was the geographical centre of Brazil. Someone thought of burying a bottle with the names of all members of the expedition. Then the party made ready to return.

On the next day, as I came up the trail, I met them trudging back towards me. Perhaps it was because I had just spent several days in the harsh light of the open river, but they looked a sickly yellow and were streaked with dirt and sweat. The rags and pans they carried barely seemed worthy of the name "possessions," and at the Centro I found Sergio and Jorge lying on the ground under a banana-leaf lean-to. We pooled the jungle fowl that *I* had shot and the jungle fowl they had shot for a joint dinner that night. Then Sergio emptied his revolver into the jatoba tree.

"What was that for, Sergio?"

"I don't know."

Together we took a few photographs to show the historic place—it looked as if a bomb had blown a large hole in the forest—and next morning we tramped back to the base camp, Sergio walking very slowly because his boots had been torn to pieces.

Nothing more happened for two days. It rained a great deal. Almost everyone spent almost all the time in their hammocks.

"Progress. Progress. Progress," Claudio said to no one in particular. "We have symbolized Progress. Our President Kubitschek has built our capital, Brasília, on the fringe of the great forest of the world. We, his officers, have carried Progress to the heart of the forest. Progress. Progress. Pooooof.

"Is Progress an extension of wealth?" Claudio went on. "Or should we achieve something more real if only for once, if only for a short time, if only for one tribe, the Indians did not die. Maybe if that happened you and I and all civilizados would have achieved something."

For fresh views on the problem I went to Rauni and asked what he thought we had been doing all these weeks in the jungle. The Txukahamae meditated for some moments. Perhaps the Caraiba, he said eventually, had lived here a long time before, had lost something, and were now looking for it. Perhaps, but he wasn't sure. It was probably a long time ago. Even before his father was born.

17

THE RAPIDS AND BELOW

SOME DAYS LATER, the expedition's four boats cruised in towards the rapids of Von Martius. "Listen," said Rauni, "the water is savage." And soon after, Sergio steered us into a reach of calm river leading towards an impressive landing of flat rocks. They seemed to form the paving of a quayside and Orlando called it "The Port of the Txukahamae."

To the east and west it was possible to see the first two hills in Xingu standing like geological sentries on either side of the river, and I remembered that at these falls an area of alluvium changed to one of metamorphosis. For hundreds of miles to the south, in the direction of Vasconcelos, the land is flat, the river winds among sandbanks, and no rocks are ever to be seen, but at Von Martius the river was said to plunge through a country of mountain and rock, off the plateau of the North Mato Grosso, and down into the basin of the Amazon. The stream would seethe with rapids, its colours would change from peaceful greens to a hurricane grey, and the sandbanks would vanish, to be replaced by great slabs of stone. This was the northern frontier of "Orlando's Cuiaba," and the great chain of falls and cascades were the reason why Xingu was, until recently, the Amazon's only unexplored tributary.

"I played here when I was little," Rauni said. "Father fishes, mother works bananas, and I play with my brothers near the water." I learned that there was a clearing for a subsidiary village and a plantation of bananas only a few minutes away, and that a two-day westward trail led from this place to the stronghold of the Txukahamae.

Rauni and Bebcuche were sent off to investigate.

An hour later, the two Txukahamae returned with an ominous report. Their heavy, primitive faces were unusually glum. There was no one about; the temporary village had not been used for a long time, and the trail to the main settlement was overgrown. In the discussion that followed, the Villas said that the deserted state of the "port" could only mean that the main village to the interior had been abandoned in another outbreak of civil war, and Orlando told us that the Txukahamae were in almost continuous fluctuation between the healing force of temporary alliance and the destructive force of internal strife. The people we wished to contact could be scattered anywhere within an area covered by the fall-out of a hydrogen bomb.

After a little more discussion, we decided to continue downstream to finish off Franklin's geological survey and then to spend what food and time remained on searching the jungle for the Txukahamae. A dump was made of most of the supplies and equipment, and, at noon next day, we set out northwards, a long line of placid water stretching out before our boats to a place where everything suddenly disappeared. The roar became louder. Our boats moved at an increasing speed.

"It's simple," Orlando said to no one in particular. "Claudio and I have been down the rapids before, and the Juruna have canoed here all their lives."

Our convoy swept forward under a heavily clouded sky. Sergio was steering in the stern of my boat, and Pitsacar, a Juruna pilot, was standing in the bows. By pointing to the left and right, he signalled us between the rocks. Orlando and Claudio looked relaxed.

"There," shouted Orlando. "Over to that stone. We must examine the falls." Immediately, the boat swooped down on a patch of rock at the very brink of the precipice where the river suddenly leaped and vanished. A calm hinterland of water sheltered us from the current, and Orlando and Claudio discussed the route, pointing out alternative passages between the rocks and foaming water.

From our position, we could see across the whole angry scene. Almost directly beneath us the water began its cascade over a stone ledge, and then it went thundering into the distance, bouncing and leaping its way down a rocky line of steps till it smoothed out 600 yards below. It was like a gigantic series of terraces that had subsided into the sea and were being lashed by a winter's storm. The course itself was about half a mile wide, studded with rocks and islands and in every way the most exciting view to be found in Xingu. There was a roar in the air; the water played as cheerfully as a cockney child. But it was hard to keep one's mind on the beauty of the scene. Cravenly, I wondered how our heavy canoes and unwieldy civilizado boats would fare when they, too, had to skip amongst the rocks and foam in adjustment to this change in the river's mood.

Fifteen minutes later, my question was answered when we cast off and Sergio steered a diagonal course across the sweeping current of the falls. In the bows, Pitsacar signalled left.

"Left," shouted Franklin, passing on the information from the middle of the boat. "Pitsacar pointed left."

"Left," said Claudio from further back, wishing to give the message the authority of his decision. "Pitsacar pointed left."

"Did you say left?" inquired Sergio, politely.

"Left," pointed Pitsacar.

"Left," said Franklin.

"Left," ordered Claudio.

To the left we moved. The boat swirled faster on to the drop, and the green of the water rapidly became a detergent white.

"Cut the motor!" shouted Orlando. "I see rocks."

"Right," signalled Pitsacar.

"Right!" shouted Franklin.

"I don't think there's any need to cut the motor," said Claudio. "I remember last year when . . ."

"What did you say?" shouted Sergio from the helm.

"Right."

"Cut."

"Don't cut."

Onwards we swept. The cataract approached. It was very large and wild.

Orlando swung round and switched off the motor.

"Now I am not so sure that you should have done that." Claudio was obviously in a reflective mood, despite the rushing onslaught of the water and the disaster we had just avoided. "The year before last I remember . . ."

Orlando leaped into the water. Pitsacar jumped after him, and soon we were all chest-high in foam, holding on to the boats. Millions of biting piumes made it unwise to lessen resistance to the current by stripping off our shirts and trousers. Boots were necessary to prevent the rocks shredding the soles off our feet. We plunged and writhed in the water.

As men shouted and struggled, Orlando ordered that one Caraiba vessel and two canoes should be left behind, each

under the charge of a man standing in a place where pro-
jecting rocks created a vacuum-like no man's land between
currents. The rest of us clung to the first boat. Ropes were
run out to Clementi and Jorge on rocks behind, and we—
the rest—heaved on the sides. With every step, someone lost
his footing and without the hold of the boat would have
soared away downstream, but somehow the joint security
of the boat, the ropes, and our feet allowed the whole con-
traption to stagger towards and on to the very lip. There the
bottom grated inch by inch over the stone, making great
spumes of water on either side. Gradually, with shouting
and floundering, and with the rope quivering under the
strain, the boat was levered over and into the lower river
beneath. Then, with Pitsacar's knowledge of the calm
stretches, we manœuvred onwards to the next brink.

In an hour and a quarter we had passed from lip to lip and
had completed the whole descent. Once during this time I
slipped and shot off—like a cork in a lavatory—downstream.
I rolled and tumbled and gasped in the water, but having
watched the others I let myself go slack and, with a little
steering, landed up in one of the currentless patches fifty
yards below. The Indians whooped and asked if I would do
it again; Rauni chased about stabbing at fish that were resting
in the calmer pools.

As we were coming down with the third boat, three or
four hours later, Claudio suddenly made me turn. I saw the
two Juruna standing upright in the little canoe that was
hissing at incredible speed on the foaming crest of the falls.
It looked like a surfboard sweeping into Honolulu. Every
now and again, one of the silhouetted figures would make a
dramatic plunge into the water with his paddle, flicking the
cockleshell away from disaster by a matter of inches.

In a few, unbelievable seconds they were floating 600
yards below on the calm of Xingu.

"It's all right with the Juruna," Claudio said, dripping

with water. "They know about rapids. But I came down
with the Txukahamae once, and they had never been in
canoes before they met Orlando and me. All the Txukahamae stood up, and I said: 'The water is too savage, isn't
it?' 'The water is more savage than a puma,' they replied,
but they whooped—and down the rapids we went.

"Perhaps it's better that way," Claudio concluded as we
staggered on to the shore. "Always, Adriano, you can make
a bark canoe afterwards."

That night, we huddled round fires trying to dry our
clothes, despite the heavy rain. At dawn, we moved off
swiftly again. Two days and several rapids later, we landed
on a small island that the rocks and speed of current made
difficult to approach. It was about thirty yards in diameter,
and piled up like a fortress with vast slabs of stone to the
height of forty feet, where a little flat platform was surrounded by a natural wall and sheltered by the island's only
tree. It was a perfect citadel from which to command the
river with rifle fire. For anyone pursued by Indians, it was
the logical place for a last stand—certainly better than the
Isle of Massacre several hours travel below, where Orlando
had found human bones and a collapsible aerial and wireless
under the sand. These had eventually been traced to an
Italian expedition searching for Fawcett.

"Oh-ho, Juruna," Orlando called out when we came to
this island. "Oh you there, Pitsacar, tell me again how these
Caraiba died and how many there were."

Pitsacar in the bows held up both hands, and then bent
two fingers away. "Eight. The Capitao," said Pitsacar, "the
cook, two soldiers, two Bakairi Indians, and two Caraiba
more."

"And the Juruna that were canoeing with them? Where
did they do?"

"They go away," said Pitsacar. "In the night they hear the

Caraiba say that they will kill the Juruna. So the Juruna—
my uncle and others—leave in the night. Next day, the
Caraiba come in their canoes and sleep here, two by the fire,
one over there by the trees, and more by the other fire. Then
the Txukahamae come with war-clubs. Boomp. Boomp.
Boomp. Two men cry and run. Boomp. Boomp. Slaughter
dead. Next day, when Juruna come, all Caraiba and Bakairi
dead."

Orlando turned to me and made the following staccato
comments. At the time of the Italian expedition the Juruna
knew nothing of the Portuguese language, and so overhearing a conversation was out of the question. It was difficult to imagine the circumstances in which a small expedition
should wish to murder its guides and protectors in the midst
of their tribal territory. How could the Juruna, who had
never spoken to the Txukahamae, know so precisely the
details of a massacre unless they themselves had been there?
Why should Rauni and Bebcuche, usually the proud claim-
ants of all tribal slaughter, be bewildered by every facet of
the story?

"Oh-ho, Juruna. Oh my friend, Pitsacar." There was a
strong tone of cynicism in Orlando's voice. As we motored
away, he debated whether the island should continue in its
name, Ilha de Massacre, or whether it should be renamed
the Island of Dysentery to commemorate more recent and
personal disasters. He was obviously in a pioneering and map-
making mood, for next day he decided that a tributary we
had discovered on the right bank should go down on the
maps of the world as the River of the Electric Eel. A
Juruna had shot one of these large, black, water creatures
earlier in the day, and Rauni had cooked it on red-hot stones
wrapped in banana leaves. Such an excellent meal! It
deserved cartographic acknowledgment.

18

SEX AND THE DYING
OF THE TRIBES

ON THE MORNING after our arrival at the River of the Electric Eel, the main party set off downstream to complete Franklin's geological survey, whilst I and four others stayed behind at a temporary base camp. A boat had been damaged in the rapids; we were to caulk it.

The days that followed at this camp were a time of unusual freedom, when we had neither rain nor duties—only the pleasure of plundering the forest for food. Our river mouth was both shrouded with trees and concealed by an island, and its course was so twisting in movement that it could have been the shape of a coiled spring. Our camp was on a hidden spit of high ground between the river and a dark lagoon. During the night, we heard alligators leaping ten yards away to the left and a restless anaconda honked just over the water to the right.

During the hours of daylight, Rauni and I would hunt

together in a canoe, beaching at the first alarm signal on shore to burst after our prey in the thick forest on either side. As game was plentiful, and this method successful, we also satisfied another craving that had been with us for several months. "We work bees today," Rauni announced on our second excursion. He carried an axe and looked up at the trees. I followed humbly with a pan. "I look for the village of the bees," he said. Then, later, stopping at a tree, "Honey live here."

There seem to be two types of honey manufacturer in Xingu, both of which nest in the hollow of a tree. The big bee has a sting, and though sometimes Rauni hacked away with a machete, screaming rather eerie laughter out into the sky every time he was attacked, the Txukahamae usually stuff the holes with burning vegetation. The other species, the small sweat bee that almost drove the expedition mad at its base camp, has no bite and makes a honey that is dark and bitter. This we extracted by axing down the tree and then tracing the course of the nest by the hollow sound it gave under a tapping machete. A panel would be cut out and Rauni, leaning in up to his shoulders, would tear out the long chain of cells whilst I held my cowboy-type felt hat with its airholes stuffed with wax from the nest. Honey poured in as the compartments were squeezed; Rauni would grin a great silky bear-like smile. "Ughhh" or "Mmmmm," he would murmur with pleasure. Finally, when everything had been torn away, he would put his hands into the trunk and drip the pools of yellow liquid that remained into his mouth and down his chin and bare tummy; he, our axes, and guns became sticky all over.

On one particular excursion, Rauni walked in the forest whilst I paddled on the river, and at his shout of discovery I ran the canoe into the nearest curve on the bank and then followed him in with an axe and gun. We chopped in turns

till suddenly, during my rest spell, Rauni turned on me, his
face black with anger.

"Why you leave my gun in the canoe?"

Unpredictable as I knew the Txukahamae to be, this took
me by surprise. "Why shouldn't I leave the gun in the
canoe?"

The tone of Rauni's reply was harsh and intolerant.
"Kuben Kran Kegn Indians come steal the gun. They kill
you and me. Then we are dead."

Standing beside our swaying "honey" tree and surrounded
by the dark vaults of the jungle, I looked at Rauni and tried
to think carefully. It was true that a trail of the Kuben Kran
Kegn tribe was meant to go through this part of the forest.
They were also the enemies of the Txukahamae. But what
were the chances of a war party striking our tiny spot during
these few unguarded moments? Infinitesimal. Still, there
the Txukahamae was, almost shaking in anger and obviously in a most dangerous mood. Rauni and I had been great
friends in the past, but I knew from the time he had tried to
kill the pilot that he was subject to sudden storms of temper.
I decided to pander to his whim.

"I will get the gun," I said, and on my return I tried one
of Orlando's sort of jokes. "There were three Kuben Kran
Kegn warriors in the canoe, Rauni. Big strong men, not
like the weak Txukahamae. They say to me: 'Take Rauni's
rifle back to Rauni. Rauni cannot hit a tapir even if it sits at
the end of his canoe. Tell him that we don't want to kill him
as he would taste like a grandfather vulture with measles.' "

Rauni laughed, and the mood vanished as inexplicably as
it had arrived. He sat down to swallow great gollops of
honey, and I took smaller and more ashamed portions as I
thought of the others in the camp. Then we wound through
the forest till a break in the bush revealed our canoe, riding
on its lianas at the edge of a little creek. Rauni sat in the

stern and I upon one leg bent under me. We paddled quietly between the rocks and snags. In the boat there was honey, our guns, some jacubim fowl shot earlier on the voyage, and a bow and arrow for tucanare. The sun was shining, the sandbanks sparkled, and Rauni sang the Txukahamae song of wild honey, a joyous "I've just eaten honey and still have some left" chant that rippled happily through the forest.

"There's an alligator," he whispered. With the bow, he fired into the water just below its eye. I watched the arrow—one of mine—move off half under the surface as if pushed by an invisible force.

"You've lost one of my arrows," I complained. "What did you do that for?"

"Alligator not good," Rauni said deeply. Then, possibly to take my mind off the loss: "Come swim. The sand here is good."

He walked in first, and I watched him prod away a sting ray that was lying amongst some sunken leaves. "Drink from here," he said diving to the bottom of the river. "The water is cold." Afterwards, we lay under the surface relaxed but careful that no part of the body was exposed to the piumes, and Rauni swung off into one of his long conversational moods.

"Tell me," he said, "you and I are friends, Adriano. Tell me, do you work women in your Cuiaba?"

"Yes," I replied. It was the answer that was needed.

"Very much?" Rauni's face glowed with expectant interest.

"Yes. Very much. And you?"

"Much too. All the time."

"With your wife?"

"No. With my wife and with other women." Rauni spoke carelessly, obviously trying to give the impression of a tribal

Don Juan. "I say to them, 'You come with me,' and afterwards I say not to tell their husbands. Husbands kill if they know. Do they kill," he said, with a kind interest in my affairs, "in your Cuiaba?"

I thought for a few minutes about our particular system. Police, divorce courts, private detectives, call girls, registry offices. I side-stepped hurriedly on to the subject of marriage in general.

"When you marry," I asked, "does your father tell you who to marry?"

"Wait there. I think." Rauni looked reflectively at the water and then went on very deliberately. "I say to girl, I like you. Then if mother like me . . ."

"What about father?"

"Father, too. Then I and girl go away to forest, and then if girl like me, we are married. I kill many pig and deer and monkey and mutum, and mother and father eat too. Then when woman has son, she stay in hut and I no kill mutum and monkey. Only others." (A reference to a sort of tabu system.)

"How tall is the girl when she marries?"

"Small when I first talk to mother." His hand indicated eight or nine. "Afterwards she this high when we marry." He indicated twelve or thirteen. "Nice," he added confidentially, "when girl like this."

Rauni then told me that he was going to take another wife as soon as he returned, and I asked if his first wife was dead.

"No," he said sadly. "Other Txukahamae talk with my wife, and afterwards she go away with him. He work woman. So I say to my brothers, 'This man has no beautifulness,' but they have fear. So I put on paint all over me and then when this man comes back to eat with his mother, I go with my war-club. His mother says, 'Why you war-club this man? He is my son and a good man.' I say, 'He has not beautifulness,' and then one runs away, two runs away, three runs away." (These I presumed were the offender's brothers, who should have fought for him.) "Then I beat," Rauni hit his own shoulder to show me. "This man falls, but there is not much how you call it?"

"Blood?" I ventured.

"Yes, blood, and afterwards he goes away to other Txukahamae."

"And your wife, Rauni?"

"She goes away too," he said grimly. "If she come back, I war-club."

"So you had no wife after that?"

"Yes, I have another, but she dies."

"No sons?"

"He die too."

I later checked the story with Bebcuche and found out that Rauni's proud statement, "I tame most times, but when other man play with me, I strong and very savage and beat with war-club," omitted the not unimportant fact that he had been supported by Bebcuche, Krumare, Mengrire, and other brothers. It seemed that in inter-tribal fights it is not permitted to strike on the head, but only on the arms and shoulders, and so Rauni's enemy had not been killed. Nor, I learned, would he have been allowed to use a knife. "Only woman. When one woman takes other woman's husband they fight with knives here," and Bebcuche had indicated his arms and mimed them pouring with blood.

. . . .

During the days that followed this conversation, I pressed Rauni to add to what I already knew of love in Xingu. Sex is a powerful influence in Indian affairs and, for an under-

standing of events in "Orlando's Cuiaba," I had to learn
something of its local expression. Particularly, I had to learn
about the Indian woman. Her position is very different from
that of the civilizada.

In a land where there is no property in the form of
privately held soil, and no possessions which cannot easily
be acquired in the forest, women are the prize of war between tribes. Their capture means child warriors and therefore tribal strength in the future; their removal can make
a group like the Suya desperate in the face of impending
extinction. In internal politics—especially amongst the
Vasconcelos Indians, where the heads of huts compete in influence and number of retainers to become recognized as
chief—daughters are important in the shuffling of forces.
After marriage, the new husband must spend six months to
one year in the house of his father-in-law, and though he has
the right to return to his own father's home, his new wife
can often persuade him to stay. Economically, the woman
plays an essential part in the division of labour. For, though
men hunt, fish, and fight, the strict rules of their position
forbid them to work in the fields—except in certain limited
functions—to carry heavy burdens, or to cook in any other
way than the hunter's method of roasting over an open fire.

Women, as the prize in war, the bribe in politics, and the
cornerstone of village economy are important in Xingu. But
this value is not reflected by their social position. Women
have no say in discussions of tribal policy; they take no
lead in ceremonies or dances; they may not dress up with
feathers or paint. Men work, but women are born to drudg-
ery. Men may rest, sport, or philosophize after the day's work
is done, but women are seldom seen away from their tasks.
Men may go anywhere, but women may not, for instance,
sit in the men's shelter at the centre of the village square.
Once when a girl of Takuman's Kamayura tribe saw some

of the sacred music instruments, she was chased into the forest and raped—tradition demanded it—by all the men.

The inferiority of womankind was brought home to me on the occasion when a man and three females landed from a canoe and I asked a Mehinaku tribesman who had arrived.

"Just a Waura," he said, giving me the name of the warrior.

He was not ignoring the women. They simply did not exist on the same plane of consideration.

If this attitude had been the sum of it all, however, sex would have played a smaller part in tribal affairs. Mr. Bertrand Flornoy has written the following judgment on the women of the Jivaro tribe in Peru: "When a woman is chosen [for marriage], she becomes bound by a chain of traditions and servile duties which she is as anxious as anyone to preserve. Her passivity and her fear of men may, on rare occasions, expose her to sexual assault which is neither rape nor adultery, since she is essentially an apathetic partner. The sexual act, devoid as it is of any sense of sin or magical significance, appears to her merely as a continuation of her household duties. She is therefore little inclined to indulge in it with anybody else than her lord and master. . . . One is forced to conclude that for the Jivaro woman, as for so many of her sex, happiness is of a purely passive order. Absence of feeling, lack of sympathy, indifference to pain, restrict her to a complacent apathy."

For the women in Xingu, the reverse seems true.

A few days after my arrival at Vasconcelos I had been sitting on a log when a young Indian man and girl came to the other end. She put her head in his lap, spoke with the thick voice of a woman approaching passion and drew his face down to tease and play with it. She did not kiss, but her poise and voice were similar to those of any European woman. She was affectionate, winning, and the complete mistress of her

man. It seemed to me that I had seldom seen more warmth
and love in such a relationship, and I later found out that this
is carried over into marriage. Then the man may be "master"
but the girl will laugh and talk as his equal, discuss his plans,
and often bend him to her will. Rauni—already the veteran
of two marriages—put it for me in this way. "Woman is a
nuisance. She say no, you Rauni mustn't travel about the forest. You stay here in the village with me and work food. She
talk, talk, all the day, like parrot bird. But I like to voyage
here and there, and I say to the woman you are a nuisance."

"But did you travel and leave her, Rauni?"

"No," he replied sadly, "I stay in the village and work."

And so, though their rights are few, Indian women exer-
cise influence through their personality and sex. Certain well-
known "grannies" are feared throughout Xingu; wives sometimes dominate their husbands; and both maidens and
matrons are constantly making trouble by the whim of their
passions. To them, infidelity is both common and easy, since
the forest is the place for sexual intercourse, whether marital
or otherwise. Though their husbands may beat and upbraid
them in public, they cannot go too far, for the wife has the
right to return to her father's hut. Secure in this last resort,
and knowing that a warrior must win the affections of his
maiden to marry her, and must preserve them to keep her as
his wife, women have a real position of strength in Xingu.
They are not mere drudges like the Jivaros for the production
of food and children, but equal partners in the endless game
of sex, whose play is as complex, incessant, and developed in
Xingu as it is in civilizado lands.

During the days at the River of the Electric Eel, Rauni told
me a great deal about sex in his tribe, and this had a bearing
both on the Indian problem and our coming search for the
Txukahamae. But what he had to say had already been put
more lucidly by Siriri, the Juruna. Once I had asked Siriri

how many children he was going to have, and he had told
me two boys and two girls.

"Why?"

"Because it's beautiful."

"And what happens if you have more?"

"I won't," he said firmly. "Juruna know a medicine. More
children is silly. Much work all the time. When woman does
not want child in stomach, she goes search in forest. You
know sipaw? Plant like sipaw. Then she drinks and then all
finished. She has child no more. You know the wife of Bimbina? She take medicine now because she no want child no
more." From Claudio I had already learned that this contra-
ceptive infusion is made from a plant not unlike the black
bean in appearance and is drunk for fifteen days—three days
on, one day off—in accordance with the menstruation cycle.
He had quoted one case in which a Kamayura woman had
five sons, then took the medicine and was without child for
ten years till she took the antidote and conceived again.

So I asked Siriri what would happen if the woman wanted
a child later.

"Woman goes look for other medicine in the forest. A leaf.
There are many at the Manitsaua-Missu. Then she passes this
on stomach." (By pass he meant rub.)

"How many times?"

"She passes one day. This leaf when long is a man leaf,
and when round is a woman leaf. If she want son she passes
man leaf, and if she want girl she passes woman leaf." I knew
that Indian oral contraceptives had been studied in English
and American laboratories and were known to be effective,
though unreliable and possibly dangerous. This, I presumed,
was an addition of superstition.

"If she has no husband," I checked, "and still uses the leaf,
does she have a child?"

"No. No child come. If she have no husband and have

child," Siriri looked serious, "father very angry. Father beats. Caraiba father in your Cuiaba beat too?" he inquired politely.

"Yes." I thought that a Caraiba father would beat too.

"You know the wife of Bimbina's son," Siriri went on. "Much time before she marry she have son in her stomach, but her mother like her very much and no tell father. Then mother beat son in the stomach, and little time after, son dead. Girl ill for many days, and her father says, 'The girl is ill.' But mother says it is only fever, and after more days girl is better. But after two moons, girl had another baby."

"But Siriri, how did the mother kill the baby? With medicine from the forest?"

"I don't know. No one knows. Only mummies. She puts hand here," he indicated his stomach, "and works. Then child dies and goes away."

"And did the mother do this the second time?"

"No. The father sees the second time. Now," Siriri said conclusively, "she is the wife of Bimbina's son."

In Xingu, though few people live over the age of forty, most villages appear to have less children under fifteen than people over that age. This seems to indicate a drop in the birth rate. But such a vague fact can do nothing more than hint at the part contraception may be playing in the dying of the Indian race. Do tribal parents, it has been asked, deliberately try to keep their children out of what they consider an unhappy world? The answer, for Xingu, is that nobody knows.

One thing is certain, however. When I asked Rauni why his tribe was divided in civil war and why we should have to search for them, he said, "Woman."

"When man want woman," he added sagely, "man fight."

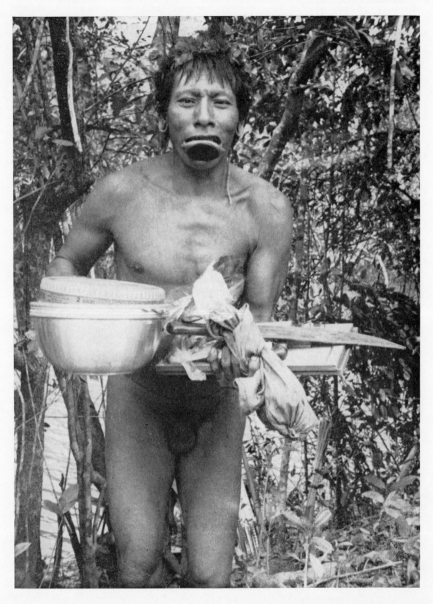

Mengrire, who was captured as a boy from the giant and unknown Kreen-Akarore tribe. He is carrying presents brought by the Villas Boas

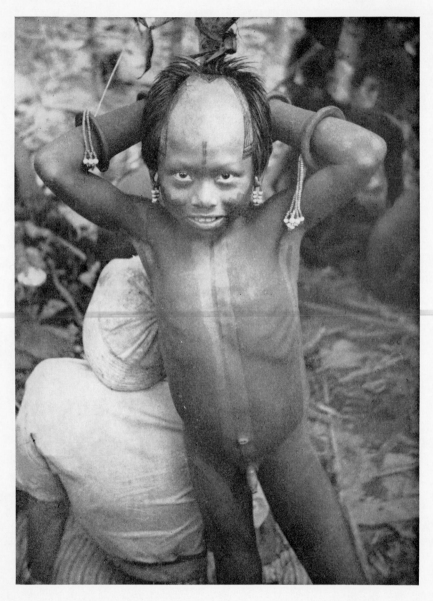

"I'm not dressed up for a dance," the boy said. "I'm just beautiful."

A mission Indian cracking and eating nuts in the forest. A nomad by tradition, he continually returns to his old way of life for months on end

An Indian raincoat

A Kamayura woman making a basket

19

MEN WHO EAT EARTH

"BOATS!" Rauni leaped from his log at the fire. "Boats," he shouted into the trees. "Two boats a long way far."

It was evening at the River of the Electric Eel, and in the sultry atmosphere Rauni's shout was as inspiring as a bugle's cry. Clementi began to pile wood on the fire, I started to pluck a pair of mutum, and the whole of our tiny camp stirred with the prospect of movement. Even the trees bending down upon us seemed to shiver with excitement. Our wait was over; the search for the Txukahamae was about to begin.

Fifteen minutes later, the main party's two boats nosed through the shadows as we hallo'd at them in the dusk, and then Orlando and the rest came ashore. Like scarecrows, they stood in a shabby line around our fire. They had reached the Serra dos Co-odenares and the geological survey was over. They had seen nothing of interest and had hurried back to make the most of the time that was left to us. They fell on our food, and when it was finished Orlando announced that departure would be at dawn next morning. Less than a week's supply of rice and beans remained, and the Txukahamae could be scattered anywhere in the vast territory of Xingu.

When we had first heard of the deserted Txukahamae village, I had wondered how the Villas would find the fragments of the tribe. Searching for wandering Indians in a trackless jungle the size of the British Isles had seemed a forlorn task, but as we listened that night to Rauni and Bebcuche talking down by the dark river front, I realized that there were several strong clues on our side. If there had been a split, it would have been along the traditional lines of tribal politics. And if the clans had separated, that of Rauni and Bebcuche—the Mentuktire—would have almost certainly returned to the hunting grounds in the east. For roughly ten years in Bebcuche's youth they had preyed on the seringueiro fringe at the Green Forest, and the route to this land lay along the River of Liberty. Somewhere—in nomadic movement beside this river—we could reasonably hope to find them.

A day later, we arrived at this tributary, on the eastern bank of the Xingu. The River of Liberty was a wide but shallow stream and our passage up it proved to be a slow and very weary process of heaving the boats over sandbanks whilst avoiding the sting rays that lay on the bottom.

By later afternoon we had reached a place where Orlando had once before contacted the faction of the Mentuktire, and there Rauni was dispatched to track his tribe.

Whilst the rest of the expedition made camp, I watched the Txukahamae take off his Caraiba shirt and Caraiba shorts and clean the blue and white beads that hung from his earlobes. He made himself a rush penis cap, bound feathers on to his forehead, and then, carrying nothing more than a .22, he strode away into the trees. In taking off his clothes he seemed to become taller and nobler in stature. I did not see him again for five days.

During this time, however, the other Txukahamae, Beb-

cuche, was very much in evidence. I would meet him wandering through the forest, a mournful figure of fantasy passing
ghostlike through the undergrowth. The two pigs that Orlando had given him had survived the long journey, the river,
the rapids, the dogs at the Juruna village, and their own inquisitive and chivalrous interest in the more dangerous things
to be found in the mysterious world of the forest. But now
that it was no longer possible to provide them with rice and
beans, they had been loosed to feed on the nuts and berries
of the jungle. Their fetters had been cut to give them a chance
against the pumas, and every day Bebcuche tracked them for
hours on end. When he found the pigs, he noted their position
and returned next morning to keep abreast with their movements.

"You see my pigs?" he would ask sadly as we met in the
quiet of the trees.

"No, Bebcuche. I am sorry. I haven't."

"No," he would mutter mournfully. "No one sees my
pigs." And then, like some Amazonian version of the Flying
Dutchman, the Txukahamae would pass me on his wistful
and endless journey.

Life was uneventful. Time passed slowly by.

On the fourth day, a canoe nosed into our camp. Mengrire, one of the great warriors of the Txukahamae, who had
originally been captured from the Kreen-Akarore, had
brought Rauni's welcome. He came with a younger man.
They stood before us noble, ambassadorial figures carrying
bows, and spoke through Bebcuche, who acted as a not very
effective interpreter.

"The tribe is not where it was before," Bebcuche trans-
lated. "It is elsewhere."

"Where?" Orlando asked.

"Over there." Bebcuche indicated a region vaguely up
river.

"Is it far?"

"No, it isn't far."

"Are the Txukahamae coming tomorrow?"

"Yes. Tomorrow."

"Do you mean tomorrow after this sleep, but before the next sleep?"

"No. They are coming tomorrow."

Bebcuche questioned Mengrire again. "Tomorrow, tomorrow," he explained lucidly.

When the whole of this next day had passed without development, we knew that the Indian inability either to appreciate or express a quantity of time meant that the Txukahamae tomorrow was an indefinite date somewhere in the future. Orlando said that the food shortage made it impossible to wait any longer. At dawn, on the morning after, we set out in the shallow-draught aluminium boat. It contained Sergio, Dilton, Bebcuche, Mengrire, the Villas, and myself.

We motored, and heaved our way over the sandbanks for several hours, as the sun poured down and the monotonous line of jungle passed on either side of our bows. Mengrire sat in front, beaming, and indicating by the sign language of two twists of his hand that the place we were seeking was round two bends of the river. Claudio was gloomy. In Indian language, he said, that could mean two spirals of the river's course and a matter of four or five miles, or two changes in the stream's direction of flow, which sometimes meant as much as a hundred miles or more. Across the linguistic barrier of our few common words, and across the great gulf between the civilizado and the Indian mind, there was no way of establishing—for certain—which it would be. An Indian understands neither time nor distance in our sense, and when travelling with him it is necessary to realize that the journey may leap without warning from two days to two months. When the forest can provide food for an endless period, and

when the Indian's own infallible sense of direction is certain
to produce the goal in the long run, he can see no need for
accurate predictions of travel data.

We continued our journey, pushing, heaving, paddling,
motoring the boat up the River of Liberty. Mengrire said that
the place was beyond some hills in the distance. When at
noon these hills were well behind us, we reflected that he
had been right; the place was indeed beyond. From my seat
I observed that Indian face watching the water and listening
to the exciting new sound of the motor, and I felt that his
mind was probably working something like this: "I, Mengrire, the great Txukahamae warrior and the guide of the
Caraiba, am happy looking at the water and listening to the
exciting new sound of the motor and reflecting that I, Mengrire, the great Txukahamae warrior . . ." And so on, round
and round in circles swirling so fast that we civilizados could
never break in upon his mind. But, quite suddenly, as if to
shame my doubts, the warrior stopped the boat at an undis-
tinguished piece of forest bank. He indicated that we should
wait, told Bebcuche in Txukahamae that the village was only
a short way away, and then—before anyone knew what was
happening—Mengrire vanished.

Half an hour later, Orlando became restless. At dinner
that night, food would run out in the main expedition camp,
and it would be four days or more till we could get back to
the dump of rice and beans above Von Martius. It was possible that the Txukahamae were preparing a special welcome for us, and also possible that this would take one or two
days to arrange. We could afford to wait no longer.

Orlando set out barefoot and, as we expected the village
to be only a few minutes away, Sergio carried the only gun.
The rest of us followed behind, a curious band, bearded, long
in the hair, and very strange in attire. My jeans were torn in
shreds from above the knee to the ankle and were held up by

a tattered leather strap which was knotted where it had broken. My shirt had half a dozen rents from the tough part of the collar to the seam in the tail and was otherwise gaudy with patches from pyjamas that had disintegrated on hunting service. My shoes had fallen to pieces. I was wearing a pair of boots three sizes too large, traded from Bebcuche who had acquired them as cast-offs from an Air Force captain. As the sole of one had come loose in the rapids and flopped up and down despite my liana bindings, I moved with a curious scraping motion.

We set out bravely. Our pace could have been described as a happy shamble.

The forest of the river bank soon gave way to bare and yellow grassland, broken every mile or two by green lines of trees that indicated wet-season watercourses. These, we discovered, were crossed by definite trails worn in the grass, and at places where water must have lain earlier in the season, we found Txukahamae huts and abandoned camp sites. Our problem was that nomad trails and makeshift dwellings such as these would be littered across the whole countryside. The technique was to guess the age of the huts and then search the next water region for a camp that was fresher, till a general line of nomadic movement could be traced; but the process did not promise quick results.

Suddenly, Bebcuche interrupted our march. "Mengrire walk here," he said, pointing at the evidence of an apparently blank patch of baked earth.

Puzzled, we looked at the empty, untrodden space. "No, no," Orlando tested. "You are wrong, my son. This is the mark of another Indian two days past going to catch fish by the river."

"Mengrire," said Bebcuche firmly. "Today."

He walked off, studying the ground, and we followed his lead.

As night came down, we were still shuffling across the

plain, and I found it hard not to remember that Claudio had once walked for twenty-eight days with even less preparation than this. Could our journey become similarly absent-minded in nature? I hoped not, and switched my thoughts to the Txukahamae. After all, the Villas and civilizados under Villas' protection were the only people ever to have met the tribe without battle. And even then there had been one occasion when some warriors had tried to kill Claudio. Now they were jumpy from internal strife, and here we were tramping to come upon them suddenly in the night. I hoped that the affair would remain as casual as it seemed.

We plodded on.

"Bebcuche." Orlando's voice was more anxious this time. "Bebcuche you have become a civilizado. Perhaps you have lived too long in Orlando's house and are following the marks of a tapir."

"Mengrire," said Bebcuche, once again pointing at blank spaces on the ground ahead. "He walk fast," he added for our benefit.

Forwards, we tramped.

Then, when it was quite dark, a faint cry was heard in the distance, and looking round I made out many torches bobbing like fishing boats in the enormous black sea of the plain. Soon, with red and ghoulish faces leaping in the flame of their rushes, with wild cries eerie in the enormous night, the Txukahamae were upon us, chests gleaming, tall, ugly, savage, but dressed in the many gorgeous colours of head feathers. As the shrieking mob swept on to us, each warrior went up in turn to Bebcuche and with one arm leaning on a bow and with his head bent over the other wrist, he shook with violent convulsions of sobbing; it was their greeting. Each man walked up to each of us in turn, and pushing his face close to, looked and let us look. Soon after a bunch of arrows was given to both Orlando and Claudio, and once again we were marching —but with Xingu's most dreaded Indians as our escort. Two young boys ran ahead carrying great bunches of flaring rushes, and leaping to either side of the path, they tore at grass and dry leaves and plunged them into the flames which they fanned in the air and held above their heads. I once looked back to see embers glowing for a long way into the distance, where torches had been dropped and were still red on the savannah. "When Txukahamae walk in the night," Bebcuche commented, "we walk like this."

An hour and a half later, the track made a twist in a patch of jungle and we were almost at the end of our search. I could see a few fires flickering in the dark. As we approached, dry rushes and leaves were piled on these to cast a red and roaring light over a scene that, in its confusion, can only be compared to a dervish dance in a foundry blast furnace. Tribes-people shouted and whirled about. A score of dogs lunged yapping to our legs. Women and children pawed at our clothes. There was a wailing generated by some emotion beyond all civilizado understanding. Primitive faces rattling lip-discs peered into mine, and then whirled away. We had leaped, quite suddenly, from the peaceful night into the noise and glare of one of the most primitive societies on earth. That society had gone berserk at our coming.

Eventually, the waves of confusion swept us into a banana-leaf hut, and we found ourselves seated on freshly cut leaves. An old woman brought a gourd of wild honey, and then three maidens—clearly the tribe's fairest—chanted a song of welcome.

In the few minutes that this gave to look about, I judged the clearing to be not much larger than an average-sized house. Within it were half a dozen lean-to huts, fifty men, women, and children, and what seemed to be an equal quantity of dogs. Then suddenly the song ceased, and the men came forward to greet the Villas—gaunt, black shapes in the flickering firelight. To give themselves importance, the men cleared the women away, who in their turn shooed the children, who, not to be outdone, attacked the dogs, who in this quite astonishing chain of pandemoniac reaction, went berserk, setting on each other in great bands, raising the night with their cries and barks. Animals, huts, and people crashed off each other like dodgem cars in a fairground.

Half an hour later, when the camp was calm once more, Rauni came up and offered us large chunks of a tapir that had been killed earlier in the day. His new wife, a very young-looking girl, was introduced, and Rauni said proudly that she had cooked the pieces on red-hot stones, reserving for us the best lumps attached by two inches of blubber to the hide. This fat was soft, and the thick hide required a great deal of tearing with the teeth to chew, so my face was soon smeared all over with grease. I asked Bebcuche if I could wash.

"Here," was the reply, "Txukahamae no wash," and he took me with a flaring torch to see the stream. It was dry, except for a hole dug out of the river-bed. Seepage had filled the cavity with a sandy concentrate of liquid, and this I drank after most of the dirt had settled to the bottom. At his turn, however, Bebcuche stirred the water round and round so that he could swallow as high a percentage of earth as possible, and I remembered that the Txukahamae are one of the few races in the world that consume earth as a regular part of their diet.

The first time I had seen anything of this had been out hunting, when Rauni had suddenly sat on the river bank and popped two large lumps of sand into his mouth. Before my interested stare, he bent over the stream and, unlike a civilizado who cups water in his palms, he made a strange flicking movement with his hands so that he could lap like a dog at the spouts and waves of liquid that rose in the air. Afterwards, he ate two more lumps.

"Is the earth good?" I asked.

"It has beautifulness," was the reply. This was accompanied by the offer of a lump, which I found unexpectedly easy to swallow and in consistency and taste very like a certain breakfast food which it would be unwise to name. Later, I found out that the Txukahamae usually consume earth in dilution with water and that some "eating earths" are regarded as better than others. The Villas presume this is due to their mineral content, which is probably also the reason for the large part that earth plays in the tribal diet.

When I returned from the stream, Claudio was dressing wounds and giving injections in one of the huts lit by the inadequate light of the fire. One of his first patients was a man with an inflamed and painful rectum.

"Too much eating earth not good," said Claudio, demonstrating theatrically how the sands rubbing would make intestines sore. "Bebcuche, tell him too much earth not good."

Bebcuche muttered away in Txukahamae and then turned back to Claudio. "Man say yes," he replied soothingly.

The man, of course, meant no, and even if it were possible to change the habit, the Villas did not wish to do so till it was known what part earth played in the diet and hence what would be needed to replace it. They had come to modify the Txukahamae way of life, but without caution there might be no Txukahamae left to modify.

As I sat, looking about that unusual scene, I did notice, however, several improvements amongst the Txukahamae. In recent centuries they had learned to use a bow; within the last hundred years, they had modified their crop system after the capture of a Juruna plantation; since 1900, they had learned to use axes, guns, and fishing line acquired from the seringueiros; and now the Villas had noticeably exploited this growing willingness to learn. Mengrire had travelled to meet us in a canoe which a Juruna under Villas' protection had shown them how to make; a small patch of rice was growing at one of the abandoned villages; Bebcuche owned two pigs; tomorrow, pots, knives, hooks, and bullets would be handed out at the boat. And above all, the Villas had once again been accepted as guests by a people which previously had friendly relations with no one. Upon this goodwill would be founded the next and most important step.

"Rauni," I had once heard Orlando say, "do you like sleeping in the hammock I have given you?"

"Yes. Sleep in hammock is good."

"Would you like me to teach the other Txukahamae how to make hammocks so that they can all have good sleep when the rain is wet on the ground? Your mother and your brothers and your wife and all the Txukahamae."

Rauni said yes.

"Will you help me to teach them, Rauni?"

"I help."

"Will you help me to teach them to make huts like the Kamayura so that when it rains the Txukahamae do not catch flu and die?"

"I help."

"Will you help me to teach them to make a proper plantation with axes and hoes, and sow beans and rice and peanuts from the Kayabi and pineapple from the Juruna?"

"I help."

The problem was to tie the nomads to some place where this instruction would be possible. The process would have to be slow to reduce the shock and would demand an end to the long wandering raids against the seringueiros and a permanent solution to the civil war.

Unfortunately, as early as Claudio's first visit to the Txukahamae, internal strife had been prevalent. One day Bebcuche, Rauni, and others of the Mentaktire had burst in on his camp, gibbering and gesticulating in concern.

Communication at that time had been limited to a few words, and so one of them had gone to Claudio's sack. He had taken out his revolver and put it in Claudio's hand.

"Other Txukahamae war-club you," the warriors both said and mimed. "When they come, you kill other Txukahamae."

Claudio, however, had put his revolver away and using the Txukahamae word for father had indicated that he could not kill his children. He had mimed his head ready for the war-club if they wished to beat it. The consternation had been complete. Eyes had rolled, tongues and lip-discs had gobbled up and down, and finally the group had rushed off to the village.

"Why Bebcuche"—I had checked on the story afterwards —"why did the Txukahamae want to kill Claudio?"

"Mentuktire, no want to kill," he said. "Only Mekragnotire."

"But why, Bebcuche, did the Mekragnotire want to kill him?"

"They no know Claudio."

"Did you fight for him?"

"No. Only my cousin kill. Krumare take war-club. Then Mengrire. Then I take club. Afterwards, other Txukahamae have fear, and afterwards they like Claudio."

That night my inquiries about the missing Mentuktire leader, Krumare, revealed some more information about the politics of the tribe. Rauni told us that Krumare and four others had made the long journey from the River of Liberty to a post on the River of Deaths, where Orlando had contacted them on a previous occasion. "They want plane to go to big Cuiaba." (Rauni meant Rio, where Orlando had once taken Krumare for a short visit to impress him with the power of the civilizado.) "Krumare want to go to big Cuiaba to get guns and bullets. Kuben Kran Kegn tribe now savage with Txukahamae. Kuben Kran Kegn have many guns and Krumare only two. But Caraiba in plane angry and say Krumare no can go."

"But Rauni," I asked, "aren't the Txukahamae strong and very many? Why is Krumare frightened?"

"Other Txukahamae go away," he told me. "And now only a few here with Krumare. Much, much sickness. Many die."

With that, Rauni went away, and I noticed that the fires were dying out. There was little movement, except from the dogs. I tried to sleep on my banana leaf, but it was hard not to wonder why a people that live and feed worse than almost any dog in London should keep an enormous canine band to increase starvation and turn their lives into anarchic bedlam. Indians have no sense of discipline, and though they beat dogs with sticks and stones on the crest of annoyance, it is not as a regular instruction to discourage crime. As a result, beating is accepted in the canine mind as an unpredictable hazard of village life; the dogs devote themselves to a career of nuisance, loitering, and burglary. They are seldom fed, and as night comes down, the skinny whelps creep between the bodies, nosing for meat and licking at unwashed lips. Occasionally, a sleeper will wake and strike at a belly passing above him. The animal screams and journeys hastily towards the jungle. The other dogs wake, and suspecting he has got away with a haunch of meat, pursue like a collectivization committee in a Russian film. The stampede is on, fast moving shapes hurtling over the sleeping bodies, till, as in my case, a dog slipped on a banana leaf and put its paw into my eye. I swung out in temper. The animal fled bleating into the dark and the stampede turned and came pouring back in my direction.

When it passed, I noticed that I was not the only one awake. Across the fire Bebcuche was sitting up on his banana leaf.

Where Rauni had left off, we started to talk.

It seemed that Krumare after his return to the Txukahamae from the post on the River of Deaths had thought of another plan. If they wouldn't let him go to Rio, perhaps they might let him fly to Vasconcelos to enlist guns and support there.

Plotting tribal war in the dimensions of aerial strategy, this astonishing Indian had set out once again on the month-long trudge to the River of Deaths.

"But Bebcuche, why don't the other Txukahamae help you?"

"They no help," Bebcuche replied logically, "because they no here. The other Txukahamae go long, lo-o-o-o-ong over there." He pointed to the west. "They live there much time now and kill many seringueiros. They have fear of us."

"Are they many?"

"Many."

"Then why do they have fear and run away from you?"

"Because before we had many Txukahamae too. We had ten houses. Now we only have five because of sickness. But the other Txukahamae have only ten men die, and so they have more than us."

"Why did they run away, Bebcuche?"

"They run because one Txukahamae take woman of other Txukahamae. Then Mekragnotire quarrel with Mentuktire. One man kill other. Before, when I small, Txukahamae fight all the time. They war-club my father dead. I cry and have anger, but this man big and I only boy, and so I cry much and do not kill."

"Is killing of one Txukahamae by another Txukahamae good?"

"Killing not good," said Bebcuche gravely, "but when men work other man's wife, then kill. Caraiba do this, I know. So Mekragnotire have much fear and go away. Mentuktire come, live here on this side of river. But after the time of rain, Krumare, Rauni, and I go search other Txukahamae. Two sleeps after village have big water." (I guessed this referred to a northern tributary of the Xingu.) "Then six more sleeps have other big water. Many Brazil nuts there." (I knew this meant a change in the type of forest.) "Then two more have

Txukahamae. We go say we savage no more. We are sad because we have no friends in our huts, only brothers. We also have fear because Kuben Kran Kegn tribe come to kill us. We ask Mekragnotire to come back to village, and we say Orlando now friend and no good kill seringueiro."

Was Bebcuche really learning? Had all these months spent with Orlando at last gained one first foothold of a victory? Or was this bit about peace and seringueiros just thrown in for my benefit?

"Then we live together," Bebcuche went on, "and sing the song of mandioca, and the song of corn and the song of water and the song of the puma and there is much beautifulness and we go slaughter all the Kuben Kran Kegn dead."

He paused for thought.

"After the rain, Adriano, you come with Krumare, Rauni, and me to the other Txukahamae? It is a long journey. Maybe, Orlando come too. Maybe you and I and Dilton and Claudio. Maybe we all voyage, long, far, over there."

"Yes," I said. "Yes, maybe." It was a thought. A thought to sleep on, I felt, as I lay beside the fire, on the banana leaf and amongst the dogs.

During the night, I woke with the drop in temperature and found that another animal—canine—was also feeling the cold. A scabby and tick-laden form lay curled between my knees and arms. Into that poor beast's happy dreams, my fist plunged like a thunderbolt. The usual cry rose deep into the night, and then towards the usual retreat the hound—as if moved by some inexorable law—departed. Like clockwork the others awoke, and the stampede was on. As I dropped off to sleep again, I reflected that if men are to be named for their outstanding characteristic, I would not have called the Txukahamae "The men who do not have a bow."

20

THE END

BY NOON on the next day, we had returned to the River of Liberty. Presents were handed out to the Txukahamae, and then, motoring, paddling, and heaving over the sandbanks, we journeyed again late into the night.

At the camp we found the expedition ready to leave, and, a few hours later, our convoy set out in mist on the long journey back to the dump at Von Martius. Our food had gone and we travelled hard. Every morning, the boats were pushed out at dawn and were motored and hauled through the rapids; we seldom beached at camp much before nightfall. The rain came down in squalls once every three or four hours, and at every break in the journey I ransacked the forest for game and fowl. Of this period, my memory records nothing at all.

Other travellers have remarked that tropical jungle seems to deaden the mind, and at this time my diary, dwindling for so long, ceases completely. Others in the expedition were similarly affected, for Franklin, the geologist, was sick with dysentery, and I often noticed Claudio staring with leaden eyes over the water, quite unconscious of the piumes and mosquitoes about him. They came in such clouds that after hunting I preferred to leave the ticks sucking at my blood than expose myself while plucking them off. But Claudio seemed anæsthetized against feeling. For half an hour on end he would sit unmoving, the few square inches on the bare part of his foot black where 300 to 400 insects were feeding on his flesh.

This "jungle sickness"—if it can be called that—affected most of us. Gradually, I came to feel that it also concerned the Indian problem.

By this last stage of the journey I had been in Xingu for seven months and was beginning to feel acclimatized to the heat and the country. Sometimes I would hunt for twelve hours without rest, bending and weaving in the undergrowth; my reactions, though still contemptible to an Indian, would have amazed my first teacher, Kaluana. But if the forest had refined the civilizado's senses, it had also dimmed the workings of his brain. Mechanical thought like "Here is some yellow jungle fruit; tapirs like this yellow jungle fruit; therefore if I wait in a tree I may shoot a tapir," still continued. But as time drew on, anything above that functional level ceased to occur. For the last month my diary was a complete blank. I seldom talked about anything except the necessary details of hunting, eating, washing, and sleeping. I did nothing but rise at dawn, stalk, kill, eat as much as I could, and then retire to a state of oblivion upon my hammock. Rivers were for canoeing on, washing in, drinking from; it certainly did not occur that they might have a view that could be looked at. The sun was to warm man after the rain; the rain a curse on earth. Previously, a few mosquitoes had been sufficient to irritate. Now they could come in hordes and hardly penetrate the apathy of a torpid mind. Not once during this time did I feel any pity for an animal before I shot it; on the other hand,

I never killed an animal for any reason but food. The mind of a civilizado was moving towards the functional brain of a hunting beast.

Looking back from the distance of half a year at this example of a civilizado in the jungle, the interesting thing seems to be the changing purpose of existence. The civilizado from England had come to Xingu for the vaguest and least commendable of reasons, but in his wish to go on an expedition, and in his interest in the Indian problem, there had been a goal beyond that of sheer survival. As the expedition drew out, this purpose swiftly disappeared. Previously, he had fidgeted at the delays in the journey and had wondered whether the hours in a hammock would drive him mad. By the end, he was pleased with every delay that meant return to that piece of cloth swinging between two trees. It was not particularly comfortable or pleasurable, but it was existence without effort.

And this life brought in its train a self-sufficiency similar to the Indian's. The civilizado no longer had any goals to achieve; he certainly did not desire to leave Xingu. If the rest of the expedition were killed, he knew that he could last as long as his cartridges and fishing line held out. Perhaps he would walk the few hundred miles to the first outpost of civilization. Perhaps he would live with the Juruna or Txukahamae. It did not really matter. He cared about nothing.

It was "jungle sickness," and the curious thing about it is that it seems to have brought the civilizado closer to the Indian. As purpose dropped out of his life and conversation, so the tribesmen appeared to become more friendly, and he seemed to have greater understanding for them. Previously, he had accepted what they said by making an effort and thinking, "This is how an Indian reacts and I must accept it because he is different." But at the last period of the expedition, no effort was needed. What the Indians said was obvious.

What they did was what ought to be done. There was a chasm between them, but as objectives and ambitions vanished from mind, so sympathy had grown for a people whose only goal was existence, and who felt a profound shock at the impact of our purposeful civilization of progress.

After a mere seven months' experience, it would be impossible to make anything but a wild guess at the Indians' way of thinking, but at the time I came to believe that I was much closer to it when I existed like a jungle man. The difference between the Indian and the civilizado is not, as it has so often been put, the three thousand years between the primitive and the modern; it is the chasm between the man who lives in the jungle and the man who lives in our civilization. And the two ways of existence imply two schools of philosophy that are hard to reconcile.

When I had first come to Xingu, I knew that the Indians were dying rapidly in Brazil and was perplexed by the comparative inactivity of the Villas Boas. They built no schools or churches; they seemed to have no program. But gradually it became clear that the Indian problem was centred round a contradiction. Desperate and vigorous measures were needed to save the tribes, and yet, because of the different nature and thinking processes of the Indian, even the most cautious and innocent action was likely to be destructive.

I had, therefore, tried to follow the Villas in probing across the chasm between the modern and primitive mind. The task had been virtually impossible, but at the end of my seven months I was guessing in what I hoped was the right direction.

"The Indian has nothing positive," Claudio had often said. "He has no ambition. He has no wish to store. No wish to improve. He relaxes within his universe. He does not struggle through it like we do."

Taking these words, I had tried to follow them through all

the aspects of Indian life, to see if this existence philosophy resulted from a need to "yield" to the forest. Gradually, I began to feel that the tribesman did not kill or store great reserves of fish and flesh simply because the jungle always provided for the man who just got up from his hammock and wandered into the limitless store-cupboard of the bush. Wealth was an impossibility to the tribesman, because everything that he possessed could be owned by any other Indian who cared to make a bow, build a hut, grind the stone head of an axe or shoot a macaw for a coloured headdress. For this reason, accumulation did not figure greatly in the tribal languages. Xavante numerals did not go on after six, and the word "six" was the same as the word for many, because, to a Xavante, six dead pigs were not very different from two hundred dead pigs. They were both too many.

My deduction was that the Indian had no ambition because he could not accumulate or conquer. He had realized that the jungle provided for its children, but destroyed those who struggled against it.

Another aspect of this trait was the tribal attitude to time. In Xingu, the longest recorded dates were two hands of moons, or "so long ago that my father told me"; this could mean anything from twenty to two thousand years before. Time to the Indian was obviously a meaningless thing. There were no events beyond birth and death, since it was the Xinguano's belief that he was his grandfather; and since the spirits of the non-incarnate dead lived below the water, time had little place in a self-perpetuating world.

Distance, too, seemed to be counted up to as many "sleeps" as there are on two hands, and beyond that everything was just a "long way away." In limitless jungle where a traveller could arrive nowhere, there could be no measurement because there was no conclusion. "Ten sleeps" was not an objective attempt to express the length of a journey, but a subjective wish to show the tiredness of the traveller. With one man, ten sleeps could be four times as far as with another.

The point behind all this was that for the Indian the jungle was so large in relation to his own powers that he did not try to measure it. The jungle's time was unceasing, and he never attempted to count it. The jungle's strength was insuperable, and he did not struggle against it. The Indian in fact had yielded to his fate, and as he could not climb out of his forest dungeon he had accepted it. The key to the whole problem was that he had made existence for its own sake the motive for his whole life. A philosophy had been constructed out of necessity, but one that had brought happiness into the forest.

Then enter we, the civilizados. Like all good liberators we tear the cage away, and the Indian, whose life has been moulded by three thousand years of acceptance of that cage, is like a man let out after a life-time of prison. The light blinds him.

Before we came, the Indian had been able to have everything that he had seen or wanted in the jungle, so that now he could not understand why he should not take the civilizado's goods. He stole. Previously the chief and the old men had been obeyed without sanction, since life outside the village was unthinkable. But now that the Indian could leave the village, the chief was ignored, and the Indian could not understand why he should be subject to a stranger's law. He had become a criminal. In the jungle village, selfishness had kept society working; care for an aged father meant insurance for one's own old age. But now that an Indian knew that the missionaries would look after him later, selfishness had had exactly the opposite effect of leading him to abandon his duties. He had lost his sense of responsibility. And so on—to the disintegration of an entire social and moral system.

Like the "liberated" so often in history, the Indian was equipped for the exact reverse of freedom. He was an un-

THE HEART OF THE FOREST

civilized man, and we said that he must be civilized. Then
we were amazed that he did not fight the challenges that
came with change. But in the forest, when the Indian was
faced with a challenge, he had previously met it by killing his
enemy. Yet we, the civilizados who were destroying him,
said that killing was wrong and refused to fight. With his
world tumbling about him, without the means of understanding the challenges, let alone having the weapons to conquer
them, the Indian despaired in his bewilderment. He had begun to lie down and die.

All this was merely the idle reasoning of a stranger to the
forest, but as the days gradually passed into months, it gave
me some sort of personal explanation or understanding of
the unlikely things that were happening.

In the first place, I realized that the ideals of our civilization were, to the jungle tribes, as lethal as bullets or epidemics.
I had often noticed whilst travelling in Brazil that, except for
the Villas, few of the people I had met who were trying
to save the Indian, had first encountered him accidentally,
then grown to like him, and finally set about a campaign to
help. Usually, they were idealists from England or Italy or
the United States who had announced that the Indian must
be saved, set out green and unknowing for the forest, and
often continued in their work, despite a growing distaste for
the animal-like and ungrateful people they were trying to
assist. The motives of their labour in the Indian problem
had nothing to do with the Indian at all, and were concerned with something deep in our own civilization. The
practice of charity had become a necessity to our Christian
existence.

In itself, this was no harmful thing, but the people who
had to save the Indian contained within themselves the very
force they were fighting against; even the best intentioned

worker in the jungle (including to a lesser extent the Villas) was a part cause of tribal destruction. He came to defend the Indian from the force of expanding economics or gold-crazy men, but brought other equally destructive facets of civilization. Usually, it was the corrosive power of aggressive idealism. What harmed the jungle man was not so much the harshness of the economic system, the ambition of evil men or the concepts of our idealistic theories, but some bustling, ruthless force that lay deep underneath in civilizado nature and which was the parent of all three. "We are right." "Preach we must." "Our cause is God's." Perhaps so, but it would seem more accurate to change the title of the subject. It was not the Indian's problem. It was ours. The tribesmen were merely victims.

As a result of these beginner's thoughts, I began to feel that I understood what had previously been the inexplicable policy of the Villas Boas. Though they had told me that a genuine solution was probably impossible, I felt, by the end of the journey, that they were better for the tribes than any of the other Indian saviours I had met in South America. For they alone had entered the forest for non-Indian and non-moral purposes. They had been paid to advance the cause of progress and to help the Central Brazilian Foundation develop the central forests of Brazil. Only after some years of living with the tribesmen had they entered the fight. Their reasons had come from friendship with the Indian himself and not from alien ideals born ten thousand miles away. The improvements they worked for were things that they had noticed the Indian wanted, not the benefits decided upon by a missionary committee of devout people in Europe or America. And above all, the Villas did not *need* success. They did not *have* to produce reports—so many new hygienic houses built, this number of souls baptized, that number of improvements made. The absence of a goal and efficient method, which infuriated so many civilizados who came to Vasconcelos, was the clue to their bond with the tribesmen.

"What do you think of Orlando and Claudio?" one of the members of our party had once asked.

"Orlando is an expedition leader, and he forgets the axes when the main purpose of our journey is to cut tracks in the forest. Salt is the only thing we really need in Xingu, because there are always fish and game to be caught. And yet, after the convoy sets out from Vasconcelos, the boats have to go back because the salt is forgotten. Do English expeditions leave nine months late? Do they drift about with no idea one day of where they are going the next?"

The answer was that though this Villas' attitude irritated civilizados, it was the basis of sympathy with the Indian who never has appointments and who hates organization and a goal. Like the Villas, the Indian knows nothing can go wrong in the jungle. After all possible disasters and the loss of every shred of equipment, the forest provides all that a primitive man can want. It is only a civilizado who must batter some prize out of the waste and who—in his hurry—often despairs and dies. To the man whose purpose is existence for its own sake, the jungle is the only home and "jungle sickness" the philosophy most suited to his environment. It is a disease only in a limited sense. On contact with civilization it leads the Indian to despair and die.

And so the fatalism or apathy of the expedition's last month seemed to round off my own doubts about Xingu. Perhaps I was beginning to think slightly like an Indian; certainly, I felt that I understood a good deal more about the Villas and the people under their charge.

Our expedition had been a strange abortion of an affair. We had started nine months late and had wasted much of our time coping with an epidemic in the Juruna village. We had cut our way to the Centro Geographico, but this had not been a particularly heroic deed, and none of us were inspired by the symbolism of our act. We had neither met nor pacified any of the wild tribes in the region; the geologist had discovered no minerals of value; our contact with the Txukahamae had only been made after weeks of wandering across the land. But none of these things had really been the point of our journey. The Villas had used the expedition to make a tour of their lands, healing the surface wounds on the Indian problem. They had neither discovered nor proposed any permanent remedy, and the whole affair had been wrapped in the complete despair of an utter tragedy. We had, however, slowed up the Indian's decline by a fraction, and, in adding to our knowledge and friendship with the tribes, had built a surer foundation for the next journey. By the weary end of the expedition, this small, unambitious, barely noticeable step forward had become a justification in itself.

Claudio and I had once, some months before, been sitting together at the Juruna village when a warrior sick with flu had walked by. He had looked the symbol of a dying tribe, and I had suddenly felt that there was more hopelessness in Claudio's life than there was in the Indians'. I had asked how any man could devote his career to a futile struggle in a lost cause.

Claudio's reply had been simple. "When civilization sweeps over these people in fifty years' time," he had said, looking very pale that morning, "they will be doomed to extinction. If we can pacify them now and prepare for the shock, perhaps we can give them a fraction of a chance. And even if we can't, Adriano, even if they are going to end, is that a reason why we should not try?"

For a few months, we had helped to try.

And thus, as the expedition forced its way up the Xingu River, it was of no concern that our journey was without a conclusion or success symbol. I sat, fatalistic, my mind a total blank. One moment of extreme rage occurred when my last boot vanished in the rapids. Then we reached the dump at Von Martius. The sacks of rice and beans were torn open, we ate, we gorged, we slept, and next morning a party led by the Villas set out to burn an airstrip close to the old Txukahamae village three days' march away. Another group of us, who had to return to our jobs and contracts, went up river to fly out to civilization. Franklin, Dilton, Raimundo, Jorge, and I made up this boat-load. To the Villas, we said a brief and hurried good-bye.

As our canoe drew away from the shore, I watched those two small, shabby figures fade into the distance and knew that for them the expedition could never be over. After the airstrip they would return to Vasconcelos, but soon they would be back. There were Txukahamae to settle, Kreen-Akarore to pacify, Kayabi to visit, Suya to look for, and other tribes to be located. As Claudio had said: "Even if they are going to end, is that a reason why we should not try?"

GLOSSARY

OF INDIAN TRIBES

Upper Xingu—"Orlando's Cuiabá"

Kamayura
Aweti
Mehinaku
Yawilapiti
Trumai } jointly referred to as Xinguanos.
Kuikuro
Kalapalo
Waura
Txikao—unpacified.
Matipuhy
Nahukua } only a few remnants—villages abandoned.
Tsuia—extinct.

Lower Xingu—The Centro Expedition

Juruna
Kayabi
Txukahamae—part of Kayapo horde and divided into the
"clans" Mentuktire and Mekragnotire.

Kreen-Akarore ⎫
Suya   ⎬ unpacified.
Miahao   ⎭

Outside Xingu

Xavante — semi-nomadic based on River of Deaths—
often raid into Xingu.

Sherente — settled in state of Goiaz—cousin tribe to
the Xavantes.

Karaja   — settled around the Ilha do Bananal.

Kuben Kran Kegn—settled across the eastern watershed of
the lower Xingu—a cousin tribe of the
Txukahamae with whom they are at present
at war.

Other tribes There are several uncontacted tribes in Xingu
known to exist on the Tapajos-Xingu water-
shed, and a tribe of "pigmies" are believed to
be somewhere between the Xingu and River
of Deaths.

A NOTE ABOUT THE AUTHOR

ADRIAN COWELL has been a traveler all his life. Born in Tungshan, China, in 1934, he was educated in Australia and England, taking his degree at St. Catharine's College, Cambridge, in 1955. While at Cambridge he and another undergraduate started an import-export company dealing in goods from Hong Kong, a company which, he is proud to say, is still flourishing. Mr. Cowell is more modest about his achievements as an explorer-anthropologist, but in a few short years he has compiled a remarkable record. In 1954 he was a member of the Trans-African Expedition sponsored jointly by Oxford and Cambridge universities, and he served as business manager for the 1955–6 Oxford-Cambridge Expedition to the Far East. In 1957–8 he joined the two universities' South American Expedition, an experience that led directly to the production of a film, *Bold Journey*, and to the writing of *The Heart of the Forest*.

January 1961